STEAM Teaching and Learning Through the Arts and Design

In this book, award-winning art educator Debrah C. Sickler-Voigt offers user-friendly, approachable strategies for STEAM planning, instruction, and assessment to help cultivate PK–12 students' full potential, and draws from wide-ranging artists and designers to help you develop inspired, creative approaches to teaching STEAM in your classroom.

Beginning with the basics and best practices of STEAM planning, instruction, and assessment, Sickler-Voigt then encourages readers to move *full steam ahead* with chapters based around diverse contemporary and historical artists and designers. In helping you to explore the interdisciplinary connections between Science, Technology, Engineering, Arts, and Mathematics, Sickler-Voigt identifies strategies to build off from STEM subjects to form authentic, well-designed, and age-appropriate learning tasks that encourage your students to make deep connections and learn subject matter in context through art media and technologies.

Each chapter includes flexible, choice-based classroom resources—with tips for adapting to different grade levels—and STEAM amplifiers, which fuse contextual learning on artists and designers with real-world STEAM topics to spark student learning and ignite creative approaches to planning, instruction, and assessment.

Featuring 150 visually stunning, full-color images, this book fuses tried-and-true best practices with highly applicable instructional models inspired by artists and STEAM professionals, ideal for PK–12 teachers and STEAM specialists.

Debrah C. Sickler-Voigt is a professor of art education at Middle Tennessee State University. She is the author of the textbook *Teaching and Learning in Art Education* (2020) and served as Senior Editor for the National Art Education Association's popular assessment papers. Her professional website is *www.arted.us*.

STEAM

Teaching and Learning Through the Arts and Design

A Practical Guide for PK–12 Educators

Debrah C. Sickler-Voigt

Routledge
Taylor & Francis Group

NEW YORK AND LONDON

Designed cover image: © Debrah C. Sickler-Voigt

First published 2023
by Routledge
605 Third Avenue, New York, NY 10158

and by Routledge
4 Park Square, Milton Park, Abingdon, Oxon, OX14 4RN

Routledge is an imprint of the Taylor & Francis Group, an informa business

© 2023 Debrah C. Sickler-Voigt

Library of Congress Cataloging-in-Publication Data
Names: Sickler-Voigt, Debrah C., 1970- author.
Title: STEAM teaching and learning through the arts and design : a practical guide for PK-12 educators / Debrah C Sickler-Voigt.
Description: New York, NY : Routledge, 2023. | Includes bibliographical references and index.
Identifiers: LCCN 2022047520 (print) | LCCN 2022047521 (ebook) | ISBN 9781032025162 (hardback) | ISBN 9781032025148 (paperback) | ISBN 9781003183693 (ebook)
Subjects: LCSH: Science--Study and teaching. | Technology--Study and teaching. | Engineering--Study and teaching. | Arts--Study and teaching. | Mathematics--Study and teaching. | Design--Study and teaching. | Interdisciplinary approach in education. | Activity programs in education.
Classification: LCC LB1585 .S498 2023 (print) | LCC LB1585 (ebook) | DDC 372.35--dc23/eng/20230125
LC record available at https://lccn.loc.gov/2022047520
LC ebook record available at https://lccn.loc.gov/2022047521

ISBN: 9781032025162 (hbk)
ISBN: 9781032025148 (pbk)
ISBN: 9781003183693 (ebk)

DOI: 10.4324/9781003183693

Typeset in Berling
by KnowledgeWorks Global Ltd.

Access the companion website: www.routledge.com/cw/sickler-voigt

Dedicated to my parents for their love, continued support, and insightful guidance in developing *STEAM Teaching and Learning Through the Arts and Design* to positively impact students' lives through the arts, design, and best teaching and learning practices.

Contents

Models

Preface

STEAM Teaching and Learning Through the Arts and Design: A Practical Guide for PK–12 Educators is a resource book for all people interested in STEAM education. It answers the common question "How do we teach STEAM (science, technology, engineering, arts, and mathematics)" through the arts and design using best and inclusive practices that recognize STEAM's subjects as coequal disciplines?" I designed this book as an independent resource in a user-friendly style for teachers' professional development. Its innovative content and context augments educators' abilities to apply the arts and design and different subjects' academic standards and terminologies to cultivate students' full potential. This book is also well suited for adoption in undergraduate and graduate courses and can be used in conjunction with my textbook Teaching and Learning in Art Education: Cultivating Students' Potential from Pre-K Through High School (ISBN-9781138549326).

As we move full steam ahead in STEAM Teaching and Learning Through the Arts and Design's seven parts, we will learn interdisciplinary/transdisciplinary approaches to STEAM planning, instruction, and assessment by aligning STEAM's subjects naturally and addressing relevant and timely issues to foster students' deep understandings. We will explore the artistic behaviors of idea development, observation, imagination and wonderment, persistence, and making creative connections to identify their relevance in STEAM education.

This book's exciting **Artists' Lessons to Thrive!** chapters present context-based narratives on historic and contemporary artists and the artistic behaviors that have informed their creative works. These chapters include choice-based lessons called **Teaching and Learning in the STEAM Artist's Studio** that offer flexibility in employing PK-12 curricular content that suits educators' and students' interests and needs and available materials and resources. Their art-making learning tasks include traditional hands-on media and integrated technologies to present a balanced, realistic, and manageable approach to instruction favored in most classrooms. The chapters' **STEAM Amplifiers** delve deeper into related interdisciplinary/transdisciplinary STEAM studies and offer inspirations to take teaching and learning in multiple directions. We will also examine educators' model applications of STEAM teaching and learning in diverse educational settings. The companion website of this book offers downloadable chapter instructional resources and image-rich PowerPoints to facilitate instruction in school, university, and community settings.

Developing the cover artwork of this book illustrates my approach to building new STEAM proficiencies. Preservice teacher Paige Brenner accompanied me in this journey as an equal partner in its development. Both of us had produced handmade tunnel books before, yet we wanted to augment our book design skills with technological applications. We participated in 3D printing, laser-cutter-engraving machine, and LED lighting trainings to integrate these technologies into our tunnel books. Their

designs include our inspirations from the ***Artists' Lessons to Thrive!*** artists and our understandings of the *STEAM Amplifiers* including balancing nature and technology. A bright sunshine and rolling hills are adorned with horses, wind turbines, and sustainable transportation. Our collaborative artmaking practices and trainings demonstrate our willingness to acquire new skills, employ STEAM standards, ask experts for help, and work through the challenges that come with creating art and trying new technologies. Richard Sickler became a welcomed member of our team with his helpful ideas for reengineering parts of our design. We reached our goals of creating informative and well-designed artworks using artistic behaviors and technological skills and can implement what we have learned in our classrooms.

Acknowledgments

STEAM Teaching and Learning Through the Arts and Design resulted from the contributions of many individuals. I thank the entire Routledge team, especially my editors. Julia Dolinger welcomed this book with enthusiasm, listened to my ideas, and applied her professional knowledge of STEAM to see it through its publication. Simon Jacobs recognized the need for this book and provided me with the creative freedom to produce an all-encompassing STEAM book. Sophie Ganesh offered her creative insights and keen attention to details in preparing this book for publication. Karen Adler welcomed me to Routledge. I am also indebted to the artists, museums, and government agencies that offered the use of images and resources. Sally Blakemore shared her wealth of knowledge, enthusiasm, friendship, and mentorship throughout the development of this book. Ed Kabotie dedicated his time and expert knowledge to teach me, make corrections, and help me grow. Litha Soyzwapi modeled exceptional professional practices and valuable life lessons. Camille Utterback extended kind and insightful communications and support. Stephan Micheletto-Blouin shared his expertise on multiple projects. Janet Echelman and Melissa Henry provided inspirational artworks and helpful feedback.

Smithsonian American Art Museum's Riche Sorenson made major contributions in supporting my research using the museum's collection. Educators in their many roles shared their expertise in teaching STEAM in schools and community settings. They include Paige Brenner, Monica Leister, James Wells, Cathy Smilan, Richard Siegesmund, Mabel Morales, Kirstie Martinez, Jenny Llewellyn-Jones, Augusto Zambrana, Patty Keller, Joshua Harper, Allen Huang, Allison Ross, Anne Henderson, Shaun Giles, Katherine Webb, Levar Robinson, Mike Mitchell, Mawish Chishty, Adriana Castro-Garcia, Kaitlyn Estes, Menley Saylor, Lucy Langworthy, Henry Lau, Iris Lau, the ICEFA Lidice team, Scratch team, Eric Breedlove, Sara Nixon, Abbey Logan, and Susanne St. John.

My family offered love and encouragement as I developed this book—especially Norbert Voigt, Pamela McColly, Richard Sickler, and Howard Dolan. Reviewers Lorinne Lee, Ryan Shin, and

Andrew Watson provided excellent feedback and shaped the early development of this book. Yichien Cooper shared her international STEAM teaching practices and offered expert feedback on the table of contents. Additional support came from Seth Feman (Frist Art Museum), Lisa Jann (L. A. Louver), Amy Sparwasser, Kathy Dumlao, Steve Cary, Hayley Moyer, Lori Santos, Jimmy Mumford, Michael Baggarly, Nancy Kelker, Paige Medlock, Ryan Vaniman, and Pattie Belsky Suzanne Pfister, and the KnowledgeWorks Global team. Valerie Hackworth, Matt Swindall, Charles Donley, Haley Hargrove, and Mohammed Bin Kulaib provided exemplary trainings and support at MTSU's James E. Walker Library Makerspace.

I warmheartedly thank the readers of *STEAM Teaching and Learning Through the Arts and Design* who will embark on this exciting adventure to apply the book's teachings and their own unique styles to make a positive difference in students' lives!

PART I

STEAM Teaching and Learning

Planning, Instruction, and Assessment

STEAM Teaching and Learning Through the Arts and Design

FIGURE 1.1 Educators learned makerspace technologies to design this STEAM-tunnel book. They brainstormed ideas, made revisions, and problem-solved to produce its design, representing STEAM's disciplines.
Source: © Debrah Sickler-Voigt, Paige Brenner, and Richard Sickler. Photo: Richard Sickler.

Welcome to our journey to move full steam ahead in teaching and learning STEAM—Science, Technology, Engineering, Arts, and Mathematics! Together we will embark on pathways to thrive and succeed. This book explains STEAM planning, instruction, and assessment for all those interested in cultivating students' full potential through a comprehensive STEAM curriculum.

DOI: 10.4324/9781003183693-2

The acts of making something special, experimenting, and studying the unknown are meaningful behaviors that have long inspired humanity (Figure 1.1). STEAM practitioners make predictions, form hypotheses, analyze data, and produce exemplary outcomes to make sense of the world and form creative solutions. Educational policies advocate for teaching a STEM/STEAM curriculum (U.S. Congress, 2015). While STEM (Science, Technology, Engineering, and Mathematics) studies are important, they do not present a full picture of what students need to know—like STEAM does, as the arts bring creativity, innovations, and design to life and enhance society's products. This book gives us access to PK-12 STEAM learning tasks that enable students to make deep connections and learn subject matter in context (Sickler-Voigt, 2020). Its choice-based curriculum provides flexibility and enables us to plan learning tasks using many of the resources we have available to us without having to rely solely on expensive technological equipment and kits—some of which may be financially out of reach.

Our focus will emphasize authentic integration that engages students in deep **interdisciplinary** STEAM studies of two or more integrated subjects that equally inform each other and **transdisciplinary** STEAM integration that holistically conjoins multiple disciplines and removes subject boundaries to deepen understandings, transform knowledge, and provide innovative solutions (Figure 1.1; Huser et al., 2020; Liao, 2016). These interwoven approaches synthesize subjects, themes, and issues to augment students' comprehensive understandings

and stimulate their minds, senses, and interests.

Participating in this chapter, we will be able to:

- Describe STEAM's disciplines.
- Explain how interdisciplinary/ transdisciplinary studies enhance STEAM teaching and learning.
- Summarize the importance of artistic behaviors in teaching STEAM.

Using this book's content, we will teach students how to create, explore, problem-solve, make revisions, and apply multiple forms of communication to study subject matter—just like artists, scientists, techies, engineers, and mathematicians do. We will also learn from artists' and designers' expert applications of design skills, media, and techniques and see how their creative works generate meaningful discourse because they communicate important ideas, appeal to our senses, and address timely issues. These 21st-century skills set students on pathways to become lifelong learners (Figures 1.2 and 1.3).

FIGURE 1.2 A pre-K student constructs and plays with stacking bricks. These behaviors serve as building blocks to develop STEAM proficiencies.

Source: Photo by Allison Shelley/The Verbatim Agency for EDUimages. (CC BY-NC 4.0).

FIGURE 1.4 Programmed LED lighting changes the STEAM-tunnel book's appearance. Its creation conjoins its five disciplines.

Source: © Debrah Sickler-Voigt, Paige Brenner, and Richard Sickler. Photo: Richard Sickler.

FIGURE 1.3 A high-school student creates a double helix sculpture. The ability to produce this artwork is grounded in foundational STEAM studies.

Source: Photo by Allison Shelley/The Verbatim Agency for EDUimages. (CC BY-NC 4.0).

STEAM'S DISCIPLINES

STEAM's individual disciplines—science, technology, engineering, arts, and mathematics—hold intrinsic values within themselves. However, when we join them together through authentic integration, we are able to see the bigger picture that illustrates the disciplines' interconnectedness and real-world applications (Figure 1.4). The following sections present an overview of the STEAM disciplines and provide foundations to participate in the interdisciplinary/transdisciplinary lessons presented in this book.

Science

Science is the study of nature and the materials that constitute all things that make up the universe. Scientists seek truth and advance knowledge and understandings about how things operate. They use **scientific inquiry** to learn facts, accumulate evidence, and make predictions through **hypotheses**—educated guesses to be investigated—about scientific phenomena that include happenings, problems, and behaviors. Scientists strive to be objective and eliminate biases through transparency. They select the best-suited methods to conduct experiments under controlled circumstances and offer scientific explanations based on empirical evidence resulting from their observations and documentation so that others can replicate and build on their work. Based on experiments, scientific **theories** provide logical explanations about how things work and why they happen. They serve as building blocks that lead to new scientific discoveries. **Laws** are observed facts that describe happenings and explain relationships between different things. Established scientific theories and laws may be challenged, disproven, changed, replaced, or evolved as new evidence and technologies arise.

Science's three branches are physical science, life science, and social science. **Physical science** is the study of nonliving entities. Its branches include chemistry, physics, and space science. Biology, ecology, and zoology are examples of **life science**, the study of living organisms in nature and their surroundings. **Social science** centers on the study of people, cultures, and societies, including sociology, psychology, and anthropology. Within this book, we will delve into artists' teachings about solar eclipses, volcanos (Figure 1.5), earthquakes (Figure 1.6), acid rain, wave formations, and severe weather (Chapters 5–7). We will learn about the biological conditions of watersheds and biological life cycle assessment (Chapters 8 and 17). We will explore neuroscience, diversity, and healthy living (Chapters 15–17).

Technology

Technology refers to scientific knowledge and advances that result in the production of tools, applications, devices, and methods to fulfill humanity's needs and wants. Technological advances extend our capabilities and productivity. Foundations of technology include computer operations, connectivity, data storage, and **coding**—computer programming in specialized languages. Computer programmers use coding to give computers and devices instructions for the tasks they are asked to perform. Manufacturers rely on technologies to speed up production and perform tasks that are too dangerous for humans. **Communication technologies** include emailing, text messaging, instant messaging, and video conferencing; whereas **assistive technologies** assist people with disabilities in performing tasks (Figure 1.7).

FIGURE 1.5 Katsushika Hokusai illustrated *Thirty-six Views of Mount Fuji*, an active volcano, including *South Wind, Clear Sky*, also known as *Red Fuji* (1830–32). Woodblock print; ink and color on paper.

Source: www.metmuseum.org. (CC0 1.0).

FIGURE 1.6 Seismologist Luke Blair teaches students at Menlo Park about earthquakes.

Source: USGS, Public Domain. Photo: Paul Lausten.

FIGURE 1.7 Preservice teachers and high school students with visual impairments utilized a 3D-printed honeycomb as an assistive technology to understand honeybees and create a stop-motion animation about honeybees.

Source: Monica Leister, Joshua Harper, and Author, teachers.

FIGURE 1.8 Jenova Chen and Kellee Santiago create video games that are beautiful artworks. Jenova Chen and Kellee Santiago, Flower, 2007, video game for SONY PS3.
Source: Smithsonian American Art Museum. © 2008 Sony Computer Entertainment American LLC. Flower is a registered trademark of Sony Computer Entertainment America LLC. Developed by Thatgamecompany.

Students readily identify video games, computers, and cellular devices as technological products. They can be surprised to learn that nonelectronic products invented long ago—including the wheel, ruler, and pencil—are technologies too. Existing technologies make way for new and emerging technologies. They improve over time by becoming more efficient—smaller, faster, and requiring less energy. Our instruction will teach students about hardware, software, and their operations as they utilize technologies to access information, research, and create. We will educate students about **digital citizenship**—avoiding harm to oneself and others when participating in technologies by communicating and acting responsibly. This book's technology lessons include digital drawing, 3D printing, video production, animation, claymation, video games (Figure 1.8), and apps (see Chapters 4, 5, 10–12, 14, and 18).

Engineering

Engineering describes human ingenuity applied to solve real-world problems using mathematical equations, scientific principles, technologies, and existing knowledge. Engineers invent, design, and construct products. They predict behaviors, identify products' and materials' extents and limitations, and check that their designs are doing what they are intended to do. Models and prototypes assist them in determining if their designs are safe and effective.

Engineering's main branches include civil engineering, mechanical engineering, electrical engineering, and chemical engineering. **Civil engineering** centers on products designed for civilian life (structures, buildings, and bridges). Civil engineers inventory existing and necessary resources to plan their designs. **Mechanical engineering** revolves around machines and mechanical systems. They span from simple machinery (wheels, levers, and screws) to complex machinery (engines, cars, and airplanes). **Electrical engineering** centers on the usage and applications of electricity and electromagnetism (electricity in magnetic fields) to develop and operate machinery, devices, and other electrical systems to solve practical problems. Examples include power, telecommunications, and computer engineering. **Chemical engineering** is the production of chemical products on a large scale for manufacturing and industry. Chemical engineers build the **reactors** that manufacture the products we use. Some develop technologies that minimize the harmful effects of chemicals and emissions (Figure 1.9).

In this book, we will learn about bots, robots, drones, bridges, architecture, marionettes, and pop-up books (Figure 1.10; Chapters 5, 8, 9, 11, 12, 15, 16, and 19). We will also identify how artists address engineering concerns including plastic pollution, wind energy, and sustainable urban design (Chapters 6 and 12).

FIGURE 1.9 Jennie C's 2020 artwork reinforces the need for chemists to design eco-friendly plastic alternatives. Grade 8, Massachusetts.
Source: NOAA Marine Debris Program. Public Domain.

FIGURE 1.10 Sally Blakemore engineers 360° pop-up books for readers to enjoy from multiple perspectives. *NASCAR Pop-Up Book: Over-the-Wall Pit Crew, 2009.*
Source: Engineered by Sally Blakemore. Illustrated by Doug Chezem. Photo: Richard Sickler.

Arts

The **arts** are acts of human expression that result in creative products and performances. Their main branches include the visual arts, performing arts, literary arts, and media arts. Each discipline utilizes specialized tools, media, and skill sets to communicate intended meanings and outcomes. The **visual arts** represent traditional fine art forms including drawing, painting, ceramics, and sculpture, as well as graphic arts, architecture, interior design, and decorative arts. **Applied arts** have functional purposes in society and may be closely associated with crafts. The **performing arts** center on music, theatre, and dance. Artists often perform in front of live audiences using instruments, objects, their bodies, and voices. The **literary arts** focus on words and language skills with artistic products that include the spoken word, poetry, creative writing, and storytelling. **Media arts** are time-based, moving products that utilize digital technologies and combine art forms including moving images, photographs, graphics, sounds, and text.

Artistic products and performances are shaped by artists' personal tastes, cultural traditions, local knowledge, and global data made available through technologies. The arts are often thought-provoking and exude emotions. **Multidisciplinary** artistic products and performances occur when artists combine art forms to produce a single work or body of works. The multidisciplinary performance of Figure 1.11 includes art robots that students designed, programmed, and constructed; an original script, and a set. Quality artworks and designs are presented throughout this book.

FIGURE 1.11 Elementary students perform their original production of *Robot World*.
Source: Fabrice Florin. Flickr, (CC by 2.0).

Mathematics

Mathematics is the scientific study of patterns and their relationships. Mathematicians study patterns to form understandings of how things work and to solve problems. Mathematical patterns have structures with repeating sequences that are found in nature, abstractions, and human inventions—including the arts (Figure 1.12). Mathematicians have invented a specialized universal language that consists of symbols and formulas. Their language is the same throughout the world. By questioning and following rules and **algorithms** (step-by-step procedures) to make calculations and predictions, mathematicians seek to make factual connections to solve problems.

Early societies invented mathematics to quantify objects and belongings. **Arithmetic** identifies basic mathematical operations that include addition, subtraction, multiplication, and division. As societies developed, people's needs for more complex mathematical solutions increased. **Algebra** applies the rules of arithmetic to solve equations using symbols to represent numbers. **Geometry** is the study of points, lines, angles, shapes, curves, planes, and solids and their relationships; whereas **trigonometry** examines triangles' lengths and angles and their relationships. **Calculus** studies the rates of changes used to create quantitative models and make predictions. People use **statistics** to collect, analyze, and interpret quantitative data to make decisions and present information.

Mathematicians apply creativity to their inquiry methods (Boaler, 2016). They ask questions, make sketches, and experiment to secure factual outcomes. Students, like mathematicians, can benefit from viewing mathematics as a dynamic subject and applying its studies to imagine diverse perspectives and possibilities. Within this book, we will learn about artists' use of algorithms, proportions, volumetric forms, charting, and mathematical calculations (Chapters 7, 10, 11, 13, 14, 16, 17, and 19). We will explore measurements, financial literacy, designing maps to scale, and aerodynamic design (Chapters 4, 6, 15, and 16).

FIGURE 1.12 Janet Echelman's *Water Sky Garden* in Vancouver, 2010, blends innovative artistic design with geometric form and mathematical patterning.
Source: Photo Christina Lazar-Schuler. (CC BY-SA), Wikimedia Commons.

ARTISTIC BEHAVIORS AND STEAM

Artistic behaviors describe the mindsets, habits, intuitions, and behaviors that artists and designers cultivate over time to inform their professional practices (Hetland et al., 2013; Sickler-Voigt, 2020). These behaviors are also shared by scientists, techies, engineers, and mathematicians. We will apply artistic behaviors as core components of our STEAM curriculum. Teaching artistic behaviors begins in early childhood and continues into adulthood. Students will learn that artists, designers, and fellow STEAM specialists ask questions, are interested in the subject matter of their times, and utilize new technologies to produce art. They apply their curiosities and research to make discoveries and understand how the universe works. Our curriculum will invite students to apply artistic behaviors as they experiment with media and processes to articulate their perspectives and make discoveries and connections. This book's featured artistic behaviors include idea development, observation, imagination and wonderment, persistence, and making creative connections.

Idea Development

The artistic behavior of idea development addresses the thoughts, refinements, and improvements to concepts and products needed to develop innovative and creative solutions. It includes experimenting, brainstorming, making revisions, independent work, and collaborations. Part II (Chapters 4–6) centers on idea development with teachings on artists Nam June Paik, Alma Thomas, and Deborah Butterfield.

Observation

Observation is the artistic behavior involving the careful and close study of objects. It includes observations from life and other data sources to acquire knowledge and form understandings. Artists and designers take inventory, notice details, see multiple perspectives, and make recordings, models, and sketches. Part III

(Chapters 7–9) focuses on observation with teachings on Katsushika Hokusai, Claude Monet, and Desert View.

Imagination and Wonderment

Imagination and wonderment is the artistic behavior that invokes artists' and designers' curiosities to know more and contemplate answers to "what if" questions. They are intrinsically motivated by their subject matter and develop products based on their interests and society's needs. Part IV (Chapters 10–13) explores imagination and wonderment with teachings on Camille Utterback, George Lucas, Jenova Chen, Kellee Santiago, and Janet Echelman.

Persistence

The artistic behavior of persistence describes how artists and designers are goal focused and work to achieve successful outcomes—even when barriers exist. They possess an inner drive and work through challenges. They make revisions and acquire data from multiple sources to generate complete understandings. Part V (Chapters 14–16) centers on persistence with teachings on Litha Soyizwapi, Jim Henson, and Sally Blakemore.

Making Creative Connections

The artistic behavior of making creative connections identifies artists' and designers' abilities to see relationships and apply creative and deductive reasoning skills to generate new knowledge and form products. They think outside of the box and make valid connections between different and/or seemingly disconnected content. Part VI (Chapters 17–19) applies making creative connections to artists' works and teaches about sites of engagement, compiled data, and going places.

YES, WE CAN TEACH STEAM!

Combining our knowledge of the STEAM disciplines with artistic behaviors, our introduction to Part I of this book, *STEAM Teaching, Learning, and Assessment*, provided us with foundational information to teach STEAM (Figure 1.13). In Chapters 2 and 3, we will augment our understandings and learn best practices for STEAM curriculum design, instruction, and assessment to build a meaningful interdisciplinary/transdisciplinary program of studies. The *Artists' Lessons to Thrive!* Chapters (4–19/Parts II–VI) feature contextual narratives, inquiry tasks, and creative applications designed to spark students' interests in STEAM (Figure 1.14). Each chapter introduces PK-12 students to its comprehensive subject matter and incorporates artistic

FIGURE 1.14 Class discussions reinforce STEAM learning in context.
Source: Photo by Allison Shelley/The Verbatim Agency for EDUimages. (CC BY-NC 4.0).

behaviors and experimentation with art media, processes, and techniques.

We can teach learning content in the exact order it appears in this book or choose the **sequence** (order of lessons) and **scope** (depth of learning) that make the best sense to us. In Part VII of this book, *Moving Full STEAM Ahead: Exciting Adventures Await Us…*, we will learn about the experiences of knowledgeable educators working within a variety of educational environments. Their noteworthy practices demonstrate teacher creativity and numerous possibilities for providing students with quality STEAM learning experiences. They reinforce our goal—"*Yes, we can teach STEAM!*"

FIGURE 1.13 This STEAM-logo design is inspired by the content of this book and reinforces how the STEAM disciplines are interconnected.
Source: © Debrah Sickler-Voigt.

MOVING FULL STEAM AHEAD...

Given this chapter's foundations in STEAM teaching and learning through the arts and design combining holistic interdisciplinary/transdisciplinary subject matter and artistic behaviors, our journey will continue in Chapter 2: Bright Ideas for STEAM Planning. We will identify goals and discover best practices to plan STEAM lessons inspired by this book's *Artists' Lessons to Thrive!* chapters. We will learn how to develop STEAM learning tasks that emphasize student choices and promote equity, diversity, and inclusion.

CHAPTER QUESTIONS AND ACTIVITIES

1. Describe the STEAM disciplines. Which of these disciplines do you feel most confident teaching and which ones seem more challenging to you?
2. What are artistic behaviors? Why are they important to STEAM education?
3. Explain how interdisciplinary/transdisciplinary methods enhance STEAM teaching and learning.

References

Boaler, J. (2016). *Mathematical mindsets: Unleashing students' potential through creative math, inspiring messages and innovative teaching.* Jossey-Bass.

Hetland, L., Winner, E., Veenema, S., & Sheridan, K. (2013). *Studio thinking 2: The real benefits of visual arts education.* Teachers College Press.

Huser, J. et al. (2020). *STEAM and the role of the arts in STEM.* State Education Agency Directors of Arts Education.

Liao, C. (2016). From interdisciplinary to transdisciplinary: An arts-integrated approach to STEAM. *Art Education, 66*(6), 44–49. doi: 10.1080/00043125.2016.1224873.

Sickler-Voigt, D. C. (2020). *Teaching and learning in art education: Cultivating students' potential from pre-K through high school.* Routledge.

U.S. Congress. (2015, December 10). *S.1177 - Every Student Succeeds Act (ESSA),* https://www.congress.gov/bill/114th-congress/senate-bill/1177/text?overview=closed

Chapter 2

Bright Ideas for STEAM Planning

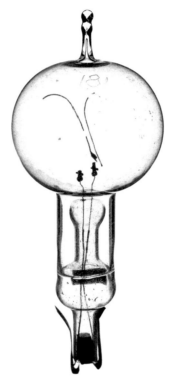

FIGURE 2.1 Thomas Alva Edison.
Edison "New Year's Eve" Lamp.
1879.
Source: Division of Work and Industry,
National Museum of American History,
Smithsonian Institution.

Bright ideas inspire us and the students we teach. We can apply Thomas Alva Edison's lightbulb (Figure 2.1) as a symbol for our bright STEAM planning, instruction, and assessment methods as we contemplate the immense possibilities available to us to implement an interdisciplinary/ transdisciplinary STEAM curriculum. Edison's persistence in refining the lightbulb and his ability to learn through trial and error resulted in his creative inventions and improvements to existing products. His innovative work in motion pictures shaped later screen technologies and influence the

DOI: 10.4324/9781003183693-3

STEAM lessons we teach, our instructional methods, and the products we use in daily life. When our curriculum is infused with STEAM's real-world applications, we teach students what it means to be inventors and creators who apply the artistic behaviors of idea development, observation, imagination and wonderment, persistence, and making creative connections.

With its emphasis on bright ideas for STEAM planning, this chapter explains the *Artists' Lesson to Thrive!* chapters' structure (Parts II–VI) and presents practical guidance to teach interdisciplinary/transdisciplinary lessons in context. It also offers methods to integrate supplemental STEAM curricular content.

Participating in this chapter, we will meet the following objectives:

- Generate skills to develop an interdisciplinary/transdisciplinary STEAM curriculum using the *Artists' Lessons to Thrive!* chapters.
- Design a curriculum rooted in equity, diversity, and inclusion.
- Provide students with choices to learn STEAM through the arts and design.

PLANNING AND THE ARTISTS' LESSONS TO THRIVE! CHAPTERS

Students are at the heart of STEAM planning. This book's *Artists' Lessons to Thrive!* chapters are designed to inspire students' imaginations, foster positive learning communities, and generate interest in learning. Their comprehensive content is rewarding for educators to teach given their many curricular choices. Their choice-based education approach originates from the textbook *Teaching and Learning in Art Education*

(Sickler-Voigt, 2020). Its model values the instinctive intuitions, behaviors, and ways of knowing that students experience when they create for personal satisfaction. Equally important, it emphasizes the necessity of students learning from knowledgeable educators who teach STEAM in context. Using its model, we will facilitate students' participation in interdisciplinary/transdisciplinary learning tasks and "ask guiding questions, teach skills, and encourage inquiry, wonderment, and exploration to foster student growth in ways unattainable without teacher guidance" (Sickler-Voigt, 2020, p. 23). Our curriculum will integrate interdisciplinary/transdisciplinary problem-based learning tasks for students to discuss relevant issues and seek creative solutions to challenges (Quigley & Herro, 2019).

The *Artists' Lessons to Thrive!* chapters begin with artists' narratives and build authentic connections between STEAM and artistic behaviors. They progress with a feature titled *Teaching and Learning in the STEAM Artist's Studio* that contains:

- a lesson introduction;
- essential and guiding questions to facilitate student inquiry;
- daily learning targets that identify student-learning tasks;
- a teaching for students' development segment that includes age-appropriate instructional methods for PK-12 students; and
- anchor standards derived from the National Core Arts Standards that identify shared skills and behaviors students will learn at all grade levels.

Each of their chapters' *STEAM Amplifiers* offer curricular choices to expand upon the *Artists' Lessons to Thrive!* content. Examples include *Measuring the*

Impacts of Acid Rain (Chapter 6); *Getting Started with Coding* (Chapter 10); and *Aerodynamic Drone Flights* (Chapter 19).

We can teach the *Artists' Lesson to Thrive!* chapters in the format they are presented in this book, as well as incorporate their content into the alternative lesson and unit plan formats we have available to us. The lesson plan *Lights, Camera, Action: Oscar and Friends Recycle!* referenced in this chapter and available on this book's companion website demonstrates an approach to expand upon the lesson of Chapter 15—*Jim Henson: Big Leaps and So Much Laughter* (Figure 2.2).

FIGURE 2.2 *Sesame Street's Oscar the Grouch Puppet* serves as an inspiration for STEAM lessons on recycling. Jim Henson (Artist), Muppets. Inc., and Eric Jacobson (Performer) *Oscar the Grouch Puppet.* 1970s.
Source: Division of Cultural and Community Life, National Museum of American History, Smithsonian Institution.

EQUITY, DIVERSITY, AND INCLUSION

Planning for equity, diversity, and inclusion (ED&I) assists us in designing a curriculum that is representative of all people. **Inclusive planning** refers to the age-appropriate learning tasks, lesson plans, and unit plans we develop so that they are fully inclusive— making our curriculum more authentic, meaningful, and balanced by incorporating the voices and contributions of all people, not just those belonging to a majority or dominant culture. We recognize that people have been marginalized, oppressed, and misunderstood for being different and work to eradicate perpetuated biases, stereotypes, and tokenism in our curriculum (Gibson, 2014; Ng et al., 2017).

This book's teachings are based on the author's research, communications, and professional interpretations of artists' and designers' works with the aim of being respectful of diversified peoples and representing their teachings in a truthful and non-biased manner. Using its *Artists' Lessons to Thrive!* chapters, our curriculum will include the powerful contributions, inspirational creations, and significant discoveries of STEAM professionals from different abilities and ethnic, religious, social, cultural, gender, and sexual orientations. Our ED&I-infused curriculum fosters students' leadership abilities and demonstrates how all people deserve equal opportunities to thrive and succeed.

GOAL SETTING

Goals shine light on what we want students to achieve. Preliminary goals prepare us for the curriculum to come. As our goals become more concrete, we will plan short- and long-term goals for students. **Short-term goals** are ones that students can achieve in short increments such as a day, week, or during a unit of study. They help students make progress as they work toward long-term goals that evolve over time and require multiple skill sets to complete. Setting long-term goals for students to learn the artistic behavior of persistence, we can make connections between Edison's persistence and puppeteer Jim Henson's persistence in convincing media executives that audiences would want to watch his Muppets. The following goals guide the *Lights, Camera, Action: Oscar and Friends Recycle!* lesson:

- Short-term goals:
  - Identify ways to reduce waste and recycle.
  - Learn how to create an instructional video/animation.
- Short- and long-term goals:
  - Recognize how people's moods can impact others.
  - Identify how my own moods can impact my behaviors and affect others.
- Long-term goals:
  - Continue to reduce waste and recycle.
  - Apply persistence to augment my existing knowledge and create additional instructional videos/animations that spark imagination and wonderment.

CHOICE-BASED STEAM LESSONS

Students desire lessons and unit plans that provide choices, such as the STEAM topics they study, their selection of materials, and the products they create. They value student-driven leadership

opportunities through which they participate in self-guided learning tasks and teach classmates. This book's companion website includes model lesson and unit plan templates to put our goals and student choices into action.

Learning Spaces and Resources

STEAM lessons identify necessary learning spaces, materials, equipment, and instructional resources. Learning occurs in classrooms, school laboratories, community venues, school and community makerspaces, students' homes, and online. We will need to inventory our available resources including materials and equipment, as well as check access to water sources and electrical outlets before instruction begins (Krakower & Martin, 2019). Special charging stations may be required when students work with electronic devices—such as a class set of tablets. Using classroom learning centers, students can share technologies, materials, and equipment. This reduces the need for whole classes simultaneously using the same resources. We may also access specialized materials and equipment through makerspaces (Figure 2.3), media centers, computer labs, and laboratory classrooms. Community spaces—such as public libraries and museums—can offer

FIGURE 2.3 Makerspace at Katz Yeshiva High School.
Source: Courtesy of kjarrett. Flickr, (CC by 2.0).

resources online and at their facilities to guide students' studies.

The Context-Driven Rationale

The *Artists' Lesson to Thrive!* narratives address timely and relevant STEAM topics. We can utilize their content to develop a context-driven lesson (or unit) **rationale** written in paragraph form that provides a descriptive overview of the lesson plan and articulates its importance within the STEAM curriculum. The rationale includes a lesson plan's academic vocabulary, essential/guiding questions, big idea(s), and objectives (see the forthcoming sections). For example, the *Lights, Camera, Action: Oscar and Friends Recycle!* rationale discusses the big idea of conservation and provides contextual information on reducing waste and recycling. It also describes how Sesame Street has been in production for over 50 years, making Oscar familiar to multiple generations. The rationale explains how moods affect others. Oscar is grouchy and can be seen as an outsider due to his pessimism. At the same time, he is funny, caring, knowledgeable, and determined. These qualities make him a relatable character as students study conservation and related STEAM subject matter in context.

Big Ideas, Enduring Understandings, and Essential Questions

Big ideas are broad topics that impact life and include artistic behaviors. They capture students' interests and build students' **enduring understandings**— knowledge that students utilize and build upon throughout their lives. We can identify the enduring understandings that drive our curriculum and reference existing ones. For example, the National Media Arts Standard (National Coalition for Core Arts Standards, 2014) enduring understanding MA:Cn11.1.—"Media artworks and ideas are better understood and produced by relating them to their purposes, values, and various contexts"— is appropriate for the *Lights, Camera, Action: Oscar and Friends Recycle!* lesson and depiction of Figure 2.4 of Oscar singing *I Love Trash*. These examples, combined with students' media artwork creations, build enduring understandings because students can apply what they learn to produce informative products that teach people about recycling. The *Artists' Lessons to Thrive!* chapters also include **essential questions** that address broad life topics and **guiding questions** that center on general issues related to lessons. The essential/guiding questions guide student inquiry about the STEAM topics identified in each chapter.

FIGURE 2.4 Sesame Street's Oscar the Grouch sings *I Love Trash*.
Source: Sesame Street YouTube Channel. "Sesame Street: I Love Trash." Fair Use.

Writing Measurable Objectives

Objectives identify measurable student behaviors and the end performances and products we expect students to attain upon completion of a lesson or unit plan. Model 2.1, "Designing Measurable STEAM Objectives," illustrates the four components of an objective: (a) the student will, (b) measurable behavior, (c) stimulus, and (d) criteria (Sickler-Voigt, 2020). Model 2.2., "Analyzing the STEAM Objective," deconstructs a model STEAM objective and describes

Model 2.1 Designing Measurable STEAM Objectives

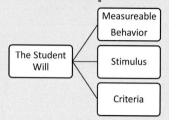

Source: *Teaching and Learning in Art Education: Cultivating Students' Potential from Pre-K Through High School* (Sickler-Voigt, 2020)

Model 2.2 Analyzing the STEAM Objective

Objective: Given an Internet scavenger hunt for recyclable products and a collection of factual data on trash reduction and recycling, students will create a puppet-production video using their original sock puppets to teach five ways to reduce the impacts of trash through recycling.

Objective Component	Description	Model Component
The Student Will	The student can be written in singular and its plural form students. It can also be identified as a group or a team.	• The students will….
Measurable Behavior	Our objective will identify one or more action verbs that will drive student behaviors and dispositions to produce measurable results.	• Create a puppet-production video.
Stimulus	The stimulus identifies instructional resources, events, data, and materials necessary for students to perform the objective.	• Given an Internet scavenger hunt for recyclable products and a collection of factual data on trash reduction and recycling. • Sock puppet.
Criteria	The criteria identify the qualities that make the objective measurable.	• Using their original sock puppets to teach five ways to reduce the impacts of trash through recycling.

each of Models 2.1's four components. It serves as a guide for writing original objectives. The majority of our objectives derived from this book's teachings will be **open-ended objectives** that provide students with curricular choices. In instances when we need to teach students particular skills, we can develop **closed-ended objectives** in which all students produce the same results. Closed-ended objectives serve as foundations to assist students in refining skills and gaining new ones as they work toward open-ended, choice-based learning tasks. For example, we might teach students how to create a cylindrical form in paper-mâché. They could later apply their knowledge to construct a galvanized-steel-styled trashcan or a recycle bin, similar to the ones Oscar the Grouch uses. Students can then apply this knowledge to design cylindrical forms for choice-based learning tasks as they construct understandings of mathematical volume and the strength of materials studied in engineering.

Daily Learning Targets

Daily learning targets use student-friendly language to break down complex objectives into smaller, more manageable parts. They assist students in reaching their desired goals. The *Artists' Lessons to Thrive!* chapters include daily learning targets that make learning tasks and anticipated performances clear to students. For example, Model 2.2's STEAM objective could be transformed into daily learning targets in the following way:

As a STEAM specialist:

- I can read about trash reduction and recycling.

- I can identify ten facts that I have learned about trash reduction and recycling and share what I know with our class.
- I can create an original sock puppet made from a repurposed sock (Figure 2.5).
- I can work with my group members to write a short script for our puppet production that identifies five ways to reduce the impacts of trash through recycling.

Given our plans for teaching the *Artists' Lessons to Thrive!* chapters, we can similarly transform their learning targets into age-appropriate measurable objectives.

FIGURE 2.5 A first-grade student presents her sock puppet.
Source: Suzanne St. John and Author, teachers. Photo: Pamela McColly.

Procedures

Procedures identify all steps within a lesson (or unit) plan from its introduction, called the set, to its closure. They identify our pre-planned instructional practices and identify student-learning tasks including group learning and independent practices. Procedures also address how we will meet students' needs as individual learners through accommodations. For example, approximately 15% of schoolchildren have special needs (U.S. Department of Education Institute of Education Sciences, 2022). We will refer to students with special needs' **individualized education programs** (IEPs) or their equivalents so that we can prepare the least restrictive environment for learning and make necessary modifications and accommodations to our lesson plans (U.S. Department of Education Individuals with Disabilities Education Act, 2006). Student populations also include gifted and talented students, students with at-risk tendencies, English language learners, and LGBTQ+ students. Some students may proceed through learning tasks more quickly than their peers and/or may also become bored if not challenged. Our planning will integrate relevant tasks, such as this book's *STEAM Amplifiers*, that encourage students to take learning to the next level without giving them the impression of busy work. When teaching students who are learning English and/or acquiring grade-level English language skills, we will plan accommodations to communicate curricular content for understanding, such as preparing informative visuals, planning class demonstrations, and breaking down the academic language. Our lessons will conclude with a closure that reinforces academic vocabulary, summarizes key concepts, and/or has students participate in class critiques. It is also an important time for cleanup.

STEAM Standards: Building Interdisciplinary/ Transdisciplinary Connections

Standards are mandated by states and local school districts and identify the learning outcomes educators expect students to achieve. They assist us in developing an age-appropriate curriculum. The *Artists' Lessons to Thrive!* chapters include the National Core Arts Standards' anchor standards. These anchor standards serve as a guide when we select grade-level **performance standards**, such as those presented in the National Visual Arts Standards and ones in our communities, to identify the competencies students are expected to know and be able to do independently at a particular grade level.

When applying an interdisciplinary/ transdisciplinary approach to curriculum design, we will incorporate standards from different STEAM subjects so that learning in each subject remains equally important with disciplinary content that comes together to provide authentic connections and deeper understandings of subject matter. **Interdisciplinary studies** address complex problems and bring real-world applications to learning. They require us to join one or more of the STEAM disciplines and their associated standards into a lesson to see relationships and foster students' deeper knowledge. Individual disciplines' boundaries dissolve. **Transdisciplinary studies** reach beyond interdisciplinary studies in that disciplines intersect, and their boundaries are fully dissolved to produce new knowledge that transcends existing possibilities. They can be achieved through comprehensive school-wide and community-based projects.

Our planning will emphasize authentic integration that engages students in deep interdisciplinary STEAM studies of two or more integrated subjects that equally inform each other and evolve to transdisciplinary STEAM integration that holistically conjoins multiple disciplines and removes subject boundaries to deepen understandings, transform knowledge, and provide innovative solutions (Huser et al., 2020; Liao, 2016). These interwoven approaches synthesize subjects, themes, and issues to augment students' comprehensive understandings and stimulate their minds, senses, and interests. This book's *Lights, Camera, Action: Oscar and Friends Recycle!* lesson includes National Core Standards for Mathematics and English Language Arts; Next Generation Science Standards for science and engineering; and ISTE National Educational Technology Standards. (Links to these standards are available on this book's companion website.) It fuses content from the individual STEAM disciplines' standards to create interdisciplinary objectives for PK-12 students. With contributions from multidisciplinary specialists, it can be broadened into a transdisciplinary unit of study.

MOVING FULL STEAM AHEAD...

This chapter provided effective methods for comprehensive, choice-based STEAM planning. It explained the *Artists' Lessons to Thrive!* chapters' content to develop interdisciplinary/transdisciplinary lesson plans that teach about artistic behaviors and promote equity, diversity, and inclusion. Referencing Edison's incandescent lightbulb and Henson's Muppets, we observed how persistence can produce positive outcomes. The *Lights, Camera, Action: Oscar and Friends Recycle!* lesson serves as a model to build upon the *Artists' Lessons to Thrive!* chapters' teachings. In the next chapter, we will augment what we have learned about interdisciplinary/transdisciplinary STEAM planning to guide our instruction and assessment practices.

CHAPTER QUESTIONS AND ACTIVITIES

1. What are your preliminary goals for teaching students a comprehensive STEAM curriculum using content from the *Artists' Lessons to Thrive!* chapters?
2. What are your plans for designing an interdisciplinary/transdisciplinary STEAM curriculum rooted in equity, diversity, and inclusion? In which environments and with which resources do you plan to teach STEAM subject matter?
3. Locate the standards used in your community to teach STEAM subjects. Analyze their content to determine strategies to build authentic interdisciplinary/transdisciplinary connections among STEAM's disciplines.

References

Gibson, P. A. (2014). Extending the ally model of social justice to social work pedagogy. *Journal of Teaching in Social Work, 34*(2), 199–214. doi: 10.1080/08841233.2014.890691.

Huser, J. et al. (2020). *STEAM and the role of the arts in STEM.* State Education Agency Directors of Arts Education.

Krakower, B., & Martin, M. (2019). *Getting started with STEAM: Practical strategies for the k-8 classroom*. Routledge.

Liao, C. (2016). From interdisciplinary to transdisciplinary: An arts-integrated approach to STEAM. *Art Education, 66*(6), 44–49. doi: 10.1080/00043125.2016.1224873.

National Coalition for Core Arts Standards. (2014). *National Core Arts Standards*. https://www.nationalartsstandards.org

Ng, W., Ware, S. M., & Greenberg, A. (2017). Activating diversity and inclusion: A blueprint for museum educators as allies and change makers. *Journal of Museum Education, 42*(2), 142–154. doi: 10.1080/10598650.2017.1306664.

Quigley, C. F., & Herro, D. (2019). *An educator's guide to STEAM: Engaging students using real-world problems*. Teachers College Press.

Sickler-Voigt, D. C. (2020). *Teaching and learning in art education: Cultivating students' potential from pre-K through high school*. Routledge.

U.S. Department of Education Individuals with Disabilities Education Act. (2006, August 14). *Sec. 300.8 Child with a Disability: Subpart A—general*. https://sites.ed.gov/idea/regs/b/a/300.8

U.S. Department of Education Institute of Education Sciences. (2022, May). *Students with disabilities*. https://nces.ed.gov/programs/coe/indicator/cgg

Chapter 3

Instruction and Assessments that Shine

FIGURE 3.1 *Armor Garniture of George Clifford, Third Earl of Cumberland* (1586). Steel, gold, leather, textile. H. 69 1/2 in. (176.5 cm).
Source: www.metmuseum.org. (CC0 1.0).

Given our strong and effective curriculum plans that gleam like skillfully-crafted armor enriched with fine details (Figures 3.1 and 3.2), we have built a solid foundation to begin STEAM instruction and assessment. Throughout this chapter, we will explore instructional practices and assessments to implement interdisciplinary/transdisciplinary curricular plans. Our aim is for

DOI: 10.4324/9781003183693-4

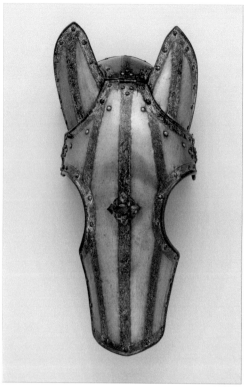

FIGURE 3.2 Shaffron (Horse's Head Defense). ca. 1620. Steel, gold, leather. H. 21 1/4 in. (54 cm); W. 10 1/4 in. (26 cm).

Source: www.metmuseum.org. (CC0 1.0).

Participating in this chapter, we will be able to:

- Identify instruction and assessment methods that make the interdisciplinary/transdisciplinary STEAM curriculum shine.
- Foster student idea development through safe and ethical inquiry-based research and creative practices.
- Balance qualitative and quantitate assessments when teaching the *Artists' Lessons to Thrive!* learning tasks.

AUTHENTIC INSTRUCTION

Authentic instruction defines how our instructional methods encourage students to want to participate in STEAM learning tasks, make personal discoveries, and form enduring understandings that have sustained value in their lives. Striving to be the best teachers we can be, we will deliver quality instruction so that students can shine as individuals and within collective groups. Implementing our interdisciplinary/transdisciplinary STEAM curriculum does not mean that we need to be perfect in each of its disciplines. As educators, some disciplines are outside of our specialized subject(s). What is most important is that we recognize that people have different strengths and remain open to trying new things—even ones with which we may initially struggle or know nothing about. This authentic-instruction approach inspired by our personal curiosities and desires to know more as lifelong learners differ from forced subject integration in which the arts and design are taught solely for the purpose of serving other disciplines—and

all parts of planning, instruction, and assessment to come together and form a unified whole that fits perfectly together like a properly-designed suit of shining armor—knowing that we are powerfully equipped with the skills and resources we need. Students are at the heart of our decisions. There is no single right way or effective means to teach, reach, and assess students. With an emphasis on authentic instruction and assessments, we will utilize established methods and theories that define best practices and balance them with the unique qualities we bring to our teaching and select effective instructional methods and assessments in alignment with the *Artists' Lessons to Thrive!* chapters.

generally lack substance (Smilan & Miraglia, 2009). As applicable, we can augment our instructional skills and curriculum by participating in professional developments and collaborating with knowledgeable partners, including peer teachers specializing in disciplines other than our own, community volunteers, and STEAM professionals.

Thinking and processing information like artists, scientists, engineers, techies, and mathematicians, our instruction teaches students how to look deeply, apply listening skills, imagine new possibilities, and try new tasks. Interactive demonstrations, multimedia teaching resources, and hands-on learning add excitement to our instruction. We will explain the value of learning tasks, review key information, and identify what comes next so that students understand what is expected of them and why it matters. Students recognize what comes easy to them and what is more challenging. Our curriculum will incorporate practice time and reviews so that students feel prepared to begin new tasks. By presenting smaller tasks that lead to bigger ones, students can better manage what they are expected to achieve and form the deep understandings necessary to reach learning targets.

We will maintain high expectations for students throughout the learning process and let them know that we believe in their capabilities while removing the pressures of having to be perfect so students can focus on the tasks at hand. Emphasizing quality over quantity assists in this regard. Students who feel safe and supported are better prepared to take risks and try new tasks. Mistakes are a natural part of the learning process. Once familiar with tasks, students will be able to perform them independently and teach others what they have learned.

Our teaching does not provide students with all of the answers so that they can explore ideas and processes independently and collaboratively, make discoveries, and build connections. For example, students can compare *Celestial Globe with Clockwork's* gilded silver and brass metals (Figure 3.3) with the steel structures and gold embellishments on the armor in Figures 3.1 and 3.2. They can determine how the materials correlate with their intended functions (see the *STEAM Amplifier* on material science and engineering in Chapter 13). Students could take learning in a new direction by comparing the constellations detailed on *Celestial Globe with Clockwork* with images captured by NASA's Hubble telescope (Figure 3.4). Additionally, they could make connections to Alma Thomas

FIGURE 3.3 Gerhard Emmoser, *Celestial Globe with Clockwork*, 1579, Partially gilded silver, gilded brass (case); brass, steel (movement), Overall: 10 3/4 × 8 × 7 1/2 in. (27.3 × 20.3 × 19.1 cm); Diameter of globe: 5 1/2 in. (14 cm). *Source: www.metmuseum.org. (CC0 1.0).*

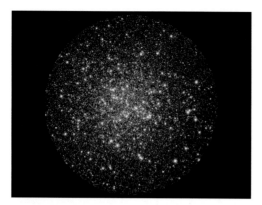

FIGURE 3.4 NASA, *Glittering Metropolis*, 2009.
Source: NASA on the Commons. NASA, ESA, and the Hubble Heritage Team (STScI/AURA). Flickr, No known copyright restrictions.

(see Chapter 5), who painted *Snoopy—Early Sun Display on Earth* and *Snoopy Sees Earth Wrapped in Sunset* (Figures 3.5 and 3.6) in response to groundbreaking photographs of the earth taken from Apollo 10's lunar module, nicknamed Snoopy. Each of these works—the armor, globe, a space photograph, and paintings of the sun shining on the earth align with the big idea shine.

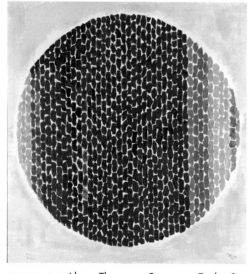

FIGURE 3.5 Alma Thomas, *Snoopy—Early Sun Display on Earth*, 1970, acrylic on canvas.
Source: Smithsonian American Art Museum, Gift of Vincent Melzac.

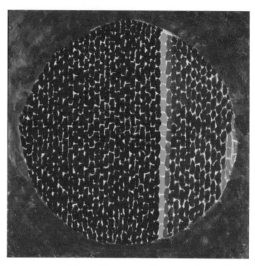

FIGURE 3.6 Alma Thomas, *Snoopy Sees Earth Wrapped in Sunset*, 1970, acrylic on canvas.
Source: Smithsonian American Art Museum, Gift of the artist.

Inquiry-Based Research

STEAM professionals use inquiry-based research methods to inform their practices. They search for facts, truth, understandings, and insights by looking closely at data and reflecting on meanings. Their inquiry methods range from fully structured and systematic to free-flowing—guided by intuition and expert knowledge. They often form hypotheses and/or make interpretations to guide their research, improve practices, and make products and processes more efficient. By thinking, processing, and researching information like STEAM professionals, students learn how to activate their minds, senses, and intuitions to interpret information. We can stimulate students' inquiry-based research skills by incorporating essential questions that center on the big ideas that drive our curriculum. Students can **brainstorm** ideas by generating lists of ideas to begin research-driven tasks. **Webbing** is an activity in which students present a core idea in a center shape. They build radiating webs of information by adding related words that extend outwards from the core idea and then move into related tangents that can guide their research on interdisciplinary/transdisciplinary STEAM subject matter. This process provides a visual record for students to reference as they determine where they want their inquiry ideas to go next. **Scavenger hunts** are exploratory searches that challenge students to discover new information. We can suggest quality resources as needed for students to begin scavenger hunts (see Chapter 8).

Research journals are spaces for students to collect data, document interview notes, make written reflections, and present relevant images such as sketches, digital photographs, and printed sources. Our instruction will teach students how to utilize journals as research tools and to refer back to journal content as their research progresses, which can include brainstorming lists, webbing charts, and results of their scavenger hunts. With continued practice, students will gain greater independence and confidence in researching STEAM and forming interdisciplinary/transdisciplinary connections.

Applying art's inquiry disciplines that include aesthetics, art criticism, art history, and visual culture, students can research diversified artists spanning different times and places and make STEAM correlations. STEAM lessons that include arts inquiry encourage students to hear other people's opinions, learn different perspectives, and develop understandings of different cultures' symbols and reasons for creating art. Through **aesthetics**, the philosophy of art, students can research and explain art's meanings (Chapters 4 and 12) and

categorize artworks (Chapter 13). **Art criticism** prompts students to describe, interpret, and evaluate art to produce informed judgments (see Chapter 7; Anderson, 1997). The *Artists' Lessons to Thrive!* chapters incorporate art historical information that adds contextual importance to STEAM teaching and learning. Studying **art history,** students learn facts and research-driven context about the history of the visual and performing arts. **Visual culture** studies invite students to examine the meanings of all types of visual images from past and present times. This book's teachings on Alma Thomas (Chapter 5), George Lucas (Chapter 11), Jenova Chen and Kellee Santiago (Chapter 12), and Jim Henson (Chapter 15) connect visual culture studies with STEAM innovations.

Studying historic armor (Figures 3.1 and 3.2) and Alma Thomas's *Snoopy* paintings (Figures 3.4 and 3.5) unite the big ideas shine and protection—as soldiers needed armor for protection in battle and astronauts use specialized equipment—including spacesuits—to conduct research in space. Like steel body armor and the spacesuit, Nick Cave designed *Soundsuits* (Figure 3.7) made from twigs,

FIGURE 3.7 Nick Cave. *Heard-NY,* 2013.
Source: Courtesy of Metropolitan Transportation Authority of the State of New York. Flickr, (CC BY 2.0). Photo by Patrick Cashin.

raffia, and found objects that he could wear as forms of protection against racial injustices (Sickler-Voigt, 2020). While knights in shining armor literally shine, people who feel safe, protected, and encouraged within a society have the ability to shine and achieve accomplishments. Asking the essential question "How does feeling protected enable people to shine and succeed?" stimulates discussions in which students add their insights and experiences to the curriculum. It is also a foundation for integrating topics including social ethics, social justice, equity, diversity, and inclusion in the STEAM curriculum.

STEAM Safety and Ethics

STEAM safety and ethics are addressed in the National Core Arts Standards and ISTE National Educational Technology Standards. Our instruction will communicate safety and ethical responsibilities in student-friendly language to build students' awareness and applications. Students will learn the importance of following directions and safety measures when using materials, tools, and equipment to avoid harm including the inhalation of particles and chemicals, ingestion of particles and small parts, and accidental cuts, crushes, and burns. We will also monitor student research to reduce potential risks. With the Internet's prominent role in education and life, we can teach students how to become aware of Internet safety guidelines and the Internet's potential risks. We can oversee students' online class communications and guide them to age-appropriate learning resources.

ASSESSMENT

Assessment measures and appraises student learning and teacher effectiveness. Valid and reliable assessments align with our goals, objectives, and student dispositions and behaviors. Many people identify STEM subjects with high-stake performances because they are often measured through **quantitative assessments** that include **paper and pencil tests** for grades and high-stake **standardized tests**. While these assessments have a purpose, students may miss the joys of the learning process when the curriculum emphasizes successful test-taking outcomes alone. Teachers assign numeric grades to students' essays, reports, presentations, and creative works. **Formative assessments**, ones utilized during learning tasks, help prepare students for quantitative assessments. They are tools for teachers and students to identify what students know and where they can improve. Using formative assessments, including **checklists** and **rubrics**, we can help students guide their own progress, move past learning barriers, make revisions, and offer them positive feedback for their achievements. At project conclusions, the scoring rubrics students utilized as formative assessments can function as summative assessments to calculate numeric grades. **Summative assessment** occurs at the end of learning tasks. Through summative assessments, we measure end results, record grades, determine if students have learned what was expected of them, and assess teaching effectiveness.

Qualitative assessments are descriptive assessments that inform us of students' dispositions and differ from quantitative assessments that measure student performances. They include meaningful discussions, teacher-student interviews, and whole-class critiques during in-progress and summative learning tasks. Qualitative assessments teach us about students' reflections on the learning process, what they have achieved, how they would like to continue to grow, and what they would like to do next. Student dispositions appraised through qualitative assessment include applications of artistic behaviors, feelings of resiliency, and informed ways of knowing about the world. They also identify the challenges students face and offer us opportunities to work with students to help them overcome obstacles. Through informal assessment, we monitor students' progress and behaviors without the intention of assigning grades.

Authentic assessments are qualitative in nature because they connect to the value of learning in everyday life and play key roles in the learning process. Grades are not their focus. Authentic assessments in STEAM teaching and learning result from interdisciplinary/transdisciplinary learning tasks that have value in life. They align with students' choice-based research, sketchbooks, capstone projects, portfolios, and community arts projects. This book emphasizes authentic practices that teach students life skills that have value in classrooms and in students' lives.

When teaching the *Artists' Lesson to Thrive!* chapters, we will balance qualitative and quantitative assessments to measure and appraise STEAM teaching and learning. For example, in developing a unit plan that teaches the big idea shine (see Chapter 5), we could quantitatively assess students' creation of a mosaic sun (Figure 3.8) and apply criteria relating to the artwork's communication of the big idea shine and the students' applications of mosaic media, effective

FIGURE 3.8 Students collaborate to design a mosaic sunshine for a school mural.
Source: Abbey Logan and Author, teachers. Photo: Pamela McColly.

production techniques, and craftspersonship. Model 3.1 illustrates how to construct a checklist with basic numeric scoring that results in a quantitative grade for the mosaic project and serves as a formative self-assessment guide for students. Teaching students how to **self-assess** as individuals and collaboratively with peers through qualitative assessments actively charges students with taking ownership of the learning process and making honest, self-reflective decisions. Qualitative assessments including student interviews and group discussions enable us to appraise students' dispositions about the learning process. Teaching the *Artists' Lessons to Thrive!* chapters, we can reference Model 3.2, as a resource to balance quantitative and qualitative assessments.

Model 3.1
Student Checklist Integrating Daily Learning Targets and Basic Scoring Assessment

Check yes or no. The project is worth up to 100 points.	Yes	No
1. We can create a mosaic sun form using multicolored glass tesserae that symbolizes the big idea shine. (70 points)		
2. We can form balanced, non-touching spaces between the mosaic tesserae that allow room for grouting. (10 points)		
3. We can use craftspersonship to apply a smooth coat of tinted grout to unify our design. (20 points)		
Total Points		

Model 3.2
Balancing Quantitative and Qualitative Assessments

Paper-pencil tests are traditional quantitative assessments with written directions that include true-false, multiple choice, matching, short answer, essay, constructed responses, fill-in-the-blank, and equations. They ask students to demonstrate knowledge of facts, procedures, and processes. Students can apply knowledge assessed on paper-pencil tests to participate in student-directed choice-based learning tasks that teachers appraise through qualitative assessment.

Research papers, **reflective essays, comparison papers,** and **artist statements** can be quantitatively assessed based on set criteria. Reflective essays and artist statements can also be used as qualitative assessments because they contain descriptors of students' thoughts, beliefs, perceived skills, and understandings.

Experiments offer students first-hand investigations of scientific and creative concepts using reasoning skills. Students perform procedures to make predictions, test theories, and explain phenomena. They apply research methods to describe, analyze, interpret, and present their results. We can assess these works quantitatively with simple numeric scoring, rubrics, and checklists. Experiments may also serve as authentic assessments with value beyond the lesson by teaching students practical research and inquiry skills.

Sketchbooks, research journals, capstone projects, and **portfolios** are creative products that consist of individual components that we can quantitatively assess. Looking at their combined works as whole products, we can apply qualitative assessments that describe students' personally driven descriptions, applications of artistic and scientific behaviors, and reflections on the learning process.

Interviews, class critiques, and student presentations emphasize students' voices. Interviews can occur between a teacher and a student and/or a small group of students. Class critiques invite students to talk about their work and the works of their peers. The products they describe may be quantitatively assessed, whereas the critique process offers qualitative feedback. Student presentations can be guided by quantitative criteria. The content students share can have personal relevance and meaning to students and be qualitatively assessed.

MOVING FULL STEAM AHEAD...

This chapter completes Part I: STEAM Planning, Instruction, and Assessment. We applied the analogies of finely-crafted shining armor and the sun in reference to the benefits of having all parts of our planning, instruction, and assessment shine and fit neatly together to provide students with quality learning experiences. Next, we will move into Part II that centers on artistic behavior of idea development. Chapter 4 on Nam June Paik introduces the first *Artists' Lessons' to Thrive!* chapter and teaches how Paik elevated video into a recognized art form.

CHAPTER QUESTIONS AND ACTIVITIES

1. How can authentic instruction and assessment enhance the interdisciplinary/transdisciplinary STEAM curriculum?
2. How will you foster student idea development through safe and ethical inquiry-based research and creative practices?
3. How will you balance qualitative and quantitate assessments when teaching the *Artists' Lessons to Thrive!* lessons?

References

Anderson, T. (1997). A model for art criticism: Talking with kids about art. *School Arts, 97*(1), 21–24.

Sickler-Voigt, D. C. (2020). *Teaching and learning in art education: Cultivating students' potential from pre-K through high school.* Routledge.

Smilan, C., & Miraglia, K. (2009). Art teachers as leaders of authentic art integration. *Art Education, 62*(6), 39–45.

PART II

Artists' Lessons to Thrive!
Idea Development

Chapter 4

Nam June Paik

Mapping the *Electronic Superhighway*

FIGURE 4.1 Nam June Paik, *Electronic Superhighway: Continental U.S., Alaska, Hawaii*, 1995, fifty-one channel video installation (including one closed-circuit television feed), custom electronics, neon lighting, steel, and wood; color, sound, approx. 15′ × 40′ × 4′.
Source: Smithsonian American Art Museum. © Nam June Paik Estate.

Nam June Paik's wall installation *Electronic Superhighway: Continental U.S., Alaska, Hawaii* exemplifies the visceral sensation of driving across the vast American landscape with moving images reminiscent of the quick glimpses of the surrounding scenery people see traveling in fast-moving cars (Figure 4.1). *Electronic Superhighway* consists of 336 vintage television sets that add significant physical weight and dimension to the installation. Paik framed its individual states with neon lights and selected location-specific content to present his interpretations of each one. Born in Korea, he arrived in the United States in 1964 and was inspired by the newly built highway system resulting from the Federal-Aid Highway Act of 1956 that made cross-country travel more accessible. *Electronic Superhighway* references American popular culture, politics, and history. Iowa flickers presidential portraits indicating its important role in American primary elections. Kansas shows the film *The Wizard of Oz*. Martin Luther King gives an anti-segregation speech in Alabama. California displays the binary code numbers 0 and 1 that provide computers with instructions. The artwork's sound clips vary from state to

DOI: 10.4324/9781003183693-6

state, like the fragmented sounds of turning the car's radio knob to find local stations. It even contains a small camera that records visitors' actions in Washington DC—making them a part of the artwork.

Paik, who studied classical music in Japan and Germany, became a prominent member of the international Fluxus movement of artists that produced highly experimental performance-based works that combined the visual arts, performances, and literature. Fluxus art emphasized conceptual ideas that challenged the established art world and focused on creative processes rather than final products. Paik's innovative ideas changed people's perceptions of television and video (Hanhardt, 2019). Film and Media Curator John Hanhardt (2006a) explained that "Paik understood that television could be an interactive and artist-empowered instrument rather than simply a one-way conduit of received programming…." For example, Paik attached high-powered magnets and electronic coils to cathode ray tube television sets to alter original network broadcast signals into abstracted performances (Hanhardt, 2006b). He broke into their casing, disassembled parts, and manipulated their circuitry to change their normative functions. By placing them sideways and upside down, he transformed television sets into sculptural objects. Together with Shuya Abe, a Japanese engineer, Paik developed the groundbreaking Paik-Abe Video Synthesizer to make further manipulations and distortions to film and video. Escalating television beyond a passive activity, he invited in-person audiences to perform with him and later used satellite transmissions to create global art performances. Digital image processors and editing enabled Paik to manipulate and layer visual data giving his works a collaged appearance (Hanhardt, 2019). He became known as the father of video art due to his ability to change society's perceptions of art.

Paik's term electronic superhighway remains relevant to fast-paced and interlinked 21st-century global technologies. He always stayed informed about the latest technologies and surrounded himself with knowledgeable collaborators who had the skills to further develop his artistic visions. Hanhardt (2019) observed: Writing and critical thinking were central to his [Paik's] life as an artist, activist, and intellectual engaged with the world around him (p. 1). For instance, Paik's 1966-written reflection demonstrates his early premonitions about what technology would become and the importance of artists in shaping future technologies: "computerized video experiments derived from the unorthodox instinct of the artist will surely bring forth some unusual results in the research of pure science and applied technology" (Hanhardt, 2019, p. 16). Given Paik's foresights and instincts about technologies, he led the way for contemporary artists to utilize technologies in ways previously unimagined and thereby facilitated society's paths down the information super highway.

Through *Teaching and Learning in the STEAM Artist's Studio 4.1*, we will invite students to participate in a mapping project in conjunction with their studies on Nam June Paik, video art, and historic pictorial maps (illustrated maps) with themes such as travel, art, plants, and global peace (Figure 4.2). The *STEAM Amplifiers* teach about conserving time-based media; cartography, satellite images, and light detection and ranging (lidar) technology; digital drawings and manipulations; and video technologies as art.

FIGURE 4.2 Ernest Dudley Chase, artist. Oliver K Whiting, publisher, circa 1944. *Mercator Map of the World United.*
Source: Norman B. Leventhal Map & Education Center at the Boston Public Library. No known copyright restrictions.

Teaching and Learning in the STEAM Artist's Studio 4.1

Introduce students to Nam June Paik and the qualities that make video an art form. Discuss the materials that Paik used to create *Electronic Superhighway.* Explain to students that when Paik arrived to the United States gasoline companies distributed free pictorial maps of tourist destinations that encouraged travelers to use their services. Given comparisons of Paik's *Electronic Superhighway* and pictorial maps (Figure 4.2 and the companion website), have students contemplate the different topics and materials they could use to create maps.

Essential/Guiding Questions

1. How did Paik's processes of idea development and experimentation inspire his creation of *Electronic Superhighway*? Why do you think Paik is considered the father of video art?
2. How do you perceive *Electronic Superhighway* most: as a map, a video performance, or an artwork? Explain your answer.

Daily Learning Targets

As an artist, I can create a map that depicts the site of my choosing. It can be a real location or one I invented.

- I can create a map key that indicates what my map's symbols mean. I can include a legend with a scale indicator and a north arrow or compass rose.
- I can select the media of my choice to create my map.
- I can design my map as a 2-D form, a puzzle, or a 3-D work.

National Core Arts Anchor Standards NVAS 1, 6, 8, and 11
www.nationalartsstandards.org

Teaching for Students' Development

PK-12: (A) Ask students to identify examples of digital media with moving images and explain how Paik's art has shaped society's understandings of media arts in everyday life (such as the Internet, gaming, and museum collections). (B) Review the characteristics of maps.

Early childhood: Young learners recognize the qualities of places they know. When introducing new locations, make associations with children's familiar sites. Teach students how to hold a camera steadily and keep images within the frame to incorporate photographs into their mapping projects.

Middle childhood: Students can work together to brainstorm topics for their maps and plan experiments like Paik. They can describe the ideas behind their work and teach others what they have learned.

Early adolescence: Middle school students prefer open-ended lessons. Encourage students to set criteria for their mapping projects and develop a checklist to identify the skills necessary to complete their project.

Adolescence: High school students can explain society's current technology needs and identify how technologies will continue to shape the human experience. Ask students to contemplate the technological needs of the future and how art can foster innovative developments.

STEAM AMPLIFIERS CHOICE #1—TIME-BASED MEDIA: ARTIST'S INTENT, CONSERVATION, AND PERFORMANCE

Paik's *Electronic Superhighway* is an example of **time-based media**, meaning it is a technology-based physical artwork that contains durational content that the artist designed with a progressive storyline. Time-based media often require exhibition spaces (Figure 4.3) for presentation and frequent care by specialized curators and conservationists due to their dependence on ever-changing technologies and equipment. They challenge established museum practices because they need updated parts to function, rather than the established tradition of salvaging an artwork's original parts. Some curators perceive the process of conserving time-based media as performances between curators, technicians, and artists because they require actions to prolong an artwork's life (Hölling, 2020; Khan Academy, 2019; Lim, 2019). Electrical technician Lee Jung-sung is part of a specialized team that conserves

FIGURE   4.3 Nam June Paik's *Electronic Superhighway: Continental U.S., Alaska, Hawaii* requires adequate exhibition spacing and care at the Smithsonian American Art Museum's Lincoln Gallery.

Source: Smithsonian American Art Museum, (CC BY-SA 3.0), Wikimedia Commons.

Paik's art. Jung-sung is referred to as Nam June Paik's hands because Jung-sung's technical knowledge brought Paik's artistic visions to life (Lim, 2019). Many media curators and technicians like Jung-sung have emphasized the importance of understanding the artist's intent in conservation work. Paik encouraged modifications to his conceptual art rather than strictly preserving their original parts and outdated technologies (Hölling, 2020). Jung-sung explained: "I once asked Mr. Paik when he was alive, 'What do we do if the TVs break down?' And he simply said, 'When that happens, we'll just replace them with ones that work'" (Lim, 2019, p. 42).

Electronic Superhighway incorporates new material, including LCD displays housed within the original television casing to maintain the artwork's sculptural form. Its digital files have replaced the original laser discs, and cracked neon lights have been exchanged with new ones. These ongoing modifications enable viewers to interact with Paik's time-based media rather than experiencing static, non-functioning artworks. Given a discussion on the conservation of time-based media, including *Electronic Superhighway*, invite students to participate in an aesthetic discussion about the qualities that make an artwork art and their perspectives on curators, conservators, and technicians replacing an artwork's original parts with newer technologies and equipment.

STEAM AMPLIFIERS CHOICE #2—CARTOGRAPHY, SATELLITE IMAGES, AND LIDAR TECHNOLOGY

Students can utilize the technological resources associated with **cartography**, the art and science of creating maps based on geographical data, to visualize geographic locations and create art. **Google Maps** and **Apple Maps** display satellite imagery, aerial photography views, street maps, and hybrid layers that combine terrain and map details. **Google Earth** takes learning to an even greater level with features that include virtual field trips, locations' background information, distance measurements, street views, and sites from multiple perspectives. Students can use it to create maps with land borders, labels, roads, transit lines, landmarks, and bodies of water.

Students can also learn how **lidar** technology has aided topographical research. Lidar is a remote sensing technology that uses light from pulsating lasers to measure the distance of ranges using a sensor to produce precise, high-definition maps that define the form and topographic elevation data (Figure 4.4). Topographic lidar measurements are usually conducted with aircraft, including drones, that house a lidar transmission unit and scan the ground. A Global Positioning System (GPS) identifies exact geographical positions (x = longitude, y = latitude, and z = altitude). Light from the scanning laser reflects back to the aircraft providing distance measurements, where the data are recorded. In addition to measuring

FIGURE 4.4 Geiger mode lidar over Chicago.
Source: U.S. Geological Survey. Public Domain. Photo: Jason Stoker.

land surfaces, lidar recognizes natural and human-made objects such as trees, buildings, monuments, and bridges.

STEAM AMPLIFIERS CHOICE #3—DIGITAL DRAWINGS AND MANIPULATIONS

Paik enriched *Electronic Superhighway* with manipulated photographs and film clips. Its designs include outlined content, geometric shapes, patterns, blocks of color, and moving bands that produce dynamic rhythms. *Electronic Superhighway's* video images are similar to digital collages with layered content that builds on each other. Students can create their own artistic manipulations of images and film stills using digital drawing apps such as Procreate, Tayasui Sketches School, and Paper by WeTransfer. Some apps offer time-lapse video recordings that show the progress of student drawings. Working with a digital stylus for touch screens, such as Apple Pencil and Stylus Logitech Crayon, assists students in adding greater details and precision to digital artworks. Students can take original pictures, as well as select existing Creative Commons images to produce a manipulated digital design that represents a story about a time and/or place. They may use a hybrid approach that combines handmade art techniques such as painting and collaging and then scan the artwork to make digital manipulations.

STEAM AMPLIFIERS CHOICE #4—VIDEO TECHNOLOGIES AS ART

Studying Paik's experimental video art performances, students can discuss the qualities that differentiate ordinary video recordings from ones that are created with the intention of being art. For example, artists experiment with different forms of lighting, camera angles, and subject matter. They can determine how dialog, sound effects, and music—or the lack thereof—add meaning to work. Paik designed video art to cause action and contemplation. An avid consumer of knowledge, Paik stayed abreast of global political happenings, environmental concerns, and issues in popular culture presented on television and in the movies (Hanhardt, 2019). Students can work in groups or independently to create video art relating to a contemporary STEAM topic, perhaps focusing on ones associated with Paik's work, including the benefits and disadvantages of technologies (Figure 4.5) and how policies shape environmental protection. Students will develop a script and storyboard to plan their video art projects. They will work with available video editing software to finalize their designs. Video editing software commonly used in education includes iMovie, Windows Video Editor, WeVideo, Final Cut Pro, and Adobe Premiere Pro.

FIGURE 4.5 This unplugged image of Nam June Paik's *Electronic Superhighway* emphasizes its sculptural form.

Source: Smithsonian American Art Museum YouTube Channel. "Nam June Paik's Electronic Superhighway— American Art Moments."

MOVING FULL STEAM AHEAD...

This chapter described how Nam June Paik's innovative ideas and experimental practices elevated video into a new art form. *Electronic Superhighway* demonstrates the interconnected roles of artist's intent, conservation, and performance in preserving time-based media. It aligns with curriculum studies on cartography, satellite images, and lidar technology and can be an inspiration for creating digital drawings and manipulating images. In the next chapter, we will continue to study the artistic behavior of idea development as we learn about the lifelong artistic pursuits of teaching-artist Alma Thomas.

References

Hanhardt, J. G. (2006a). Chance in a lifetime: John G. Hanhardt on Nam June Paik. *Artforum, 44*(8), 51–54.

Hanhardt, J. G. (2006b). Nam June Paik (1932–2006). *American Art, 20*(2), 148–153.

Hanhardt, J. G. (2019). The textual worlds of Nam June Paik: The time of writing and reading. In H. G. Hanhardt, G. Zinman, & E. Decker-Phillips (Eds.), *We are in open circuits: Writings by Nam June Paik* (pp. 1–19). MIT Press.

Hölling, H. B. (2020, May 25). Archival activations: The writings of Nam June Paik. *Metropolis M,* 2. https://www.metropolism.com/en/features/40893_archival_activations_writings_of_nam_june_paik

Khan Academy. (2019). *Preserving Nam June Paik's Electronic Superhighway.* [Video]. https://www.khanacademy.org/humanities/art-1010/conceptual-and-performance-art/conceptual-performance/v/nam-june-paik-electronic-superhighway

Lim, H. (2019). The man called 'Nam June Paik's hands'. *Koreana, 33*(2), 38–43.

Chapter 5

Alma Thomas

Beyond a Shadow of a Doubt

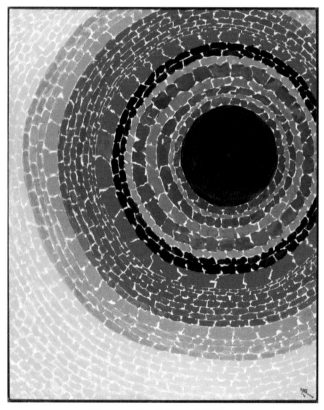

FIGURE 5.1 Alma Thomas, *The Eclipse*, 1970, acrylic on canvas.
Source: Smithsonian American Art Museum, Gift of the artist.

Alma Thomas dedicated her life to the acquisition of knowledge, creating art, and helping others. She is credited as becoming an artist in her 70s and 80s after retirement as an art teacher. While this story forms an interesting narrative, Thomas's artistic pursuits span her entire lifetime (Feman, 2021). Education was important to Thomas's family. They relocated from Georgia with its oppressive Jim Crow laws to Washington, D.C. so that Thomas could pursue a high-school education and study art, which directed her professional life's course (Munro, 1979; Smithsonian Institution Archives of American Art, 2019). She was the first person to earn a fine art degree from Howard University. Thomas also received a Master of Art Education from Columbia

DOI: 10.4324/9781003183693-7

University and further developed her painting skills at American University.

As a **teaching artist** who taught for 40 years, Thomas expressed "I devoted my life to the children and they loved me" (Munro, 1979, para. 6). Her role as an educator contributed to her artistic development, as demonstrated in her lifelong pursuit of knowledge and skill refinement. She applied her studio skills and arts advocacy to her instruction. Thomas's curriculum encouraged black students, who experienced segregation in Washington D.C., to "go into integrated spaces and experience them. Own the city and claim the city" (S. Feman, personal communication, May 13, 2022). Thomas lived by this practice. A consummate thinker and creator of ideas, she was surrounded by art professionals, pursued leadership roles in the arts, and facilitated opportunities for artists of color in her community. Aware of the racial tensions, violence, and segregation in her lifetime, Thomas chose to make positive changes as an educator and used her art to inspire others: "Through color I have sought to concentrate on beauty and happiness in my painting rather than on man's inhumanity to man" (Smithsonian Institution Archives, 2019, p. 7).

Color is a prominent feature in Thomas's cutting-edge *Space Series* that highlights scientific phenomena and achievements.

The Eclipse (Figure 5.1) was inspired by the 1970 total solar eclipse over Washington D.C. Thomas painted the eclipse in a concentric circle design with the moon represented as its dark blue central form surrounded by sunlight painted as dynamic brushstrokes, called **Alma's stripes**, that radiate outward from the moon. *The Eclipse's* warm colors suggest the glow of the **solar corona**, the gases that form the outermost region of the sun's atmosphere. Her circular designs and rainbow colors, which Thomas explained symbolize peace (Smithsonian Institution Archives, 2019), can serve as analogies for bringing diverse people together—as people form learning, social, and support circles. Beyond a shadow of a doubt, Thomas's lifelong pursuits achieved remarkable outcomes given her role as a teaching artist with a body of works and instructional practices that demonstrate how bright and beautiful an inclusive world can be.

Applying *Teaching and Learning in the STEAM Artist's Studio 5.1's* content, we will teach students about Thomas and explain how her work connects to **astronomy**—the scientific study of the universe of beyond the earth's atmosphere including celestial objects like the sun, moon, stars, and planets. The *STEAM Amplifiers* include solar eclipses, sun safety, engineering marionette productions, and stop-motion animations.

Teaching and Learning in the STEAM Artist's Studio 5.1

Explain to students how Alma Thomas's lifelong pursuits influenced the teaching artist she became. She pulled from the contemporary artistic and scientific innovations of her time to develop a unique painting style exemplified through her Alma's stripes. Ask students to make comparisons to Alma's stripes and other artists' mark-making applications and color palettes to identify how stylistic changes impact the appearances and meanings of art.

Essential/Guiding Questions

1. Thomas proclaimed "I have always been interested in this rapid changing world, the 20th century machine and space ages" (Smithsonian Institution Archives, 2019, p. 34). In your opinion, why was it important for Thomas to formulate her ideas about scientific phenomena and beauty into artworks including *The Eclipse*?
2. What does lifelong learning mean to you? How did Thomas demonstrate lifelong learning?

Daily Learning Targets

As an artist, I can create an artwork inspired by astronomy in the artistic style of my choice.

- I can create artistic marks that add meaning to my choice of subject matter. I can select the best art media to produce my marks.
- I can choose the colors that represent my ideas.
- I can present my completed artwork, describe its meaning, and explain how I produced its design. I can summarize one or more facts about its astronomical subject matter.

National Core Arts Anchor Standards NVAS 3, 5, 7, and 10
www.nationalartsstandards.org

Teaching for Students' Development

PK-12: (A) Present a sampling of mark-making techniques and color palettes that artists use to communicate meaning. (B) Introduce astronomy to students and explain how it inspired Thomas's *Space Series*.

Early childhood: Young children are learning how to make marks with art supplies. Demonstrate the proper ways to hold art supplies and have students practice making marks with different media.

Middle childhood: Students have further developed their fine motor skills and can make more controlled marks. Demonstrate color mixing so students can produce a broader array of colors.

Early adolescence: Middle school students can mix a wider color palette and produce varied marks. Encourage students to experiment and produce original marks that showcase their artistic styles.

Adolescence: High school students apply metacognitive skills when creating art. Ask students to identify a personally-driven concept—like Thomas did with beauty—that has significant meaning to them and incorporate it into their design through color and mark making.

STEAM AMPLIFIERS CHOICE #1—THE SOLAR ECLIPSE

When presenting Thomas's *The Eclipse*, teach students that a **solar eclipse** is a celestial phenomenon that occurs when a new moon is positioned between the sun and earth. The moon temporarily blocks the sun's rays from reaching portions of the earth, which are blanketed by the moon's shadow. Eclipses do not occur with each new moon due to the moon's different rotational angle tilted away from the earth's rotation around the sun. Therefore, the moon's shadow does not reach the earth. While the sun and moon appear to be the same size, the sun is 400 times larger than the moon. The moon is 400 times closer to the earth than the sun making it appear equally as large as the sun.

The moon's alignment with the sun and earth determines the type of solar eclipse. A **total solar eclipse** occurs when the moon covers the sun in its entirety. The portions of the earth covered by the moon's **umbra shadow**, which is dark and small in size, experience the total eclipse because the moon completely blocks out the sunlight. The umbra shadow's movement across the earth's surface is called the **path of totality**. A large **penumbra** shadow surrounds the umbra shadow that is lighter in color because some of the sunlight in those positions of the earth have visible sunlight. Watching a total solar eclipse, spectators witness its exciting changing effects as the sun's disk becomes partially covered and then fully covered by the moon when the total eclipse occurs. The sun's corona glows around the moon's form. After the total eclipse, the sun disk gradually reappears until it reaches its entirety (see Figure 5.2).

FIGURE 5.2 This image documents the phases of a total solar eclipse.
Source: NASA/Aubrey Gemignani. Public Domain.

A **partial eclipse** conceals only a fraction of the sun with parts of the sun remaining exposed. It is located outside of the path of totality in the penumbra shadow. The sun appears to have a crescent form. An **annular eclipse**, meaning ring of fire, takes place when the moon is centrally positioned directly in front of the sun. The moon's orbital location is too far away and cannot conceal the entire sun. It looks like a surrounding ring around the moon and produces a brighter eclipse. The final eclipse is a **hybrid eclipse**, also known as an **annular-total eclipse**, because parts of the earth's surface have an annular eclipse, while other regions experience the total eclipse. The moon is further away for those seeing the annular eclipse, while the parts of the earth in the umbra shadow witness a total solar eclipse.

STEAM AMPLIFIERS CHOICE #2—WE PRACTICE SUN SAFETY!

When viewing a solar eclipse, people can become so excited that they want to look at it with their bare eyes. Looking directly at a solar eclipse without certified protective eyewear, even briefly, may cause **solar retinopathy** that results from ultraviolet solar radiation entering the eyes and irritating retinal (eye lens) tissue. Damaging effects include eye pain, vision distortion, seeing altered colors, central vision loss, and blind spots. People can only look safely at an eclipse without certified eye protection during the brief moments that it is fully eclipsed.

Referencing Thomas's *The Eclipse*, we will teach students that people need to practice sun safety even on days without a solar eclipse (Figure 5.3). Sunglasses protect people's eyes from Ultraviolet A and Ultraviolet B (UV) rays. Wearing SPF (sun protection factor) 30+ sunblock and reapplying it every two hours and after swimming, toweling off, or sweating prevent burns and damage that can cause skin cancer resulting from too much exposure to the sun's ultraviolet light. Reflective water, snow, and sand also increase the chances of sunburn. Wearing protective clothing that covers the skin and a brimmed hat help prevent sunburns. We will explain the importance of seeking shaded areas when sitting and playing outdoors on hot days. It is also important to drink plenty of water to prevent dehydration. Before heading outdoors, students can look at the UV index that predicts the level from 1–11+ to determine the strength of UV rays.

FIGURE 5.3 The sun's ultraviolet rays minimize at sunset; however, people can experience eye damage when staring directly at the sun.
Source: © Richard Sickler.

STEAM AMPLIFIERS CHOICE #3—ENGINEERING STAR-STUDDED MARIONETTES

In 1934, Alma Thomas participated in puppeteer Tony Sarg's intensive summer marionette theatre class. Thomas learned Sarg's methods including engineering marionettes, weighting marionette figures so that they could balance and move freely, operating controllers, and constructing and painting puppetry stage and scenery. Thomas taught these skills to her students at Shaw Junior High School. Her teaching and community advocacy broke barriers because she secured opportunities for her students to be invited to perform their marionette productions at racially segregated venues including festivals, local schools, and community centers (Walz, 2021).

Marionette productions offer students exciting opportunities to apply engineering skills. Chen et al. (2004) explained "From the engineering perspective, the marionette is a wire- (or string-) driven multi-limbed under-actuated mechanism under gravity influence that exhibits rich kinematic and dynamic behaviours" (p. 119). To operate smoothly, a suspended marionette's mechanical design needs to have a balanced weight distribution. The puppeteer manipulates the attached strings, which function as actuators responsible for moving the jointed body parts so that they appear to have lifelike motions. Students can refer to Sarg's illustrations (Figure 5.4) that demonstrate how to string marionettes with attachments at the head, wrists, and knees to design marionette productions. They can perform scripts about the solar eclipse and other astrological phenomena.

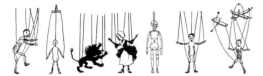

FIGURE 5.4 These marionette-engineering illustrations come from *The Tony Sarg Marionette Book*, 1921. Thomas participated in Tony Sarg's marionette theatre class.

Source: Cornell University Library, Internet Archive. Public Domain. Compilation: Paige Brenner.

STEAM AMPLIFIERS CHOICE #4—STOP-MOTION ANIMATIONS AND CLAYMATIONS

Students have many choices to develop out-of-this-world stop-motion animations and claymations. **Stop motion animation** is the process of photographing frame-by-frame incremental movements of non-moving objects to capture a sequential series of events and give the appearance of movement. Stop motion animation provides students with creative flexibility using multimedia including photography, audio, and film and traditional art-making processes. Students can create stop-motion animations on apps such as Stop Motion Studio Pro and work solely within the apps or make final edits in a movie program, such as iMovie.

Claymation refers to the process of modeling characters and other objects with plasticine clay to produce stop-motion animations (Figure 5.5). When teaching claymation, demonstrate how to construct an armature from aluminum foil and wire to reduce the amount of plasticine needed to create figures. An armature also makes the claymation characters lighter and easier to move. Claymation figures require a larger and heavier base for balance and stability.

Students' astronomy-inspired scripts can be purely factual or fictionalized with integrated factual information. Invite students

FIGURE 5.5 A student forms a honey-bee claymation character for a scene showing a NASA image as its backdrop.

Source: Monica Leister, Joshua Harper, and Author, teachers.

to examine Thomas's *Space Series* (including Figures 3.5, 3.6, and 5.1) carefully to learn their subject matter. Then have students search NASA's and The National Park Service's (Figure 5.6) public domain

FIGURE 5.6 Images like this solar eclipse from Great Sand Dunes National Park and Preserve can be helpful resources for creating STEAM-inspired animations.

Source: NPS/Patrick Myers. Flickr, Public Domain Mark 1.0.

high-resolution astronomical photographs and videos as inspirations to create artistic backdrops and props for their sets. They can also utilize them to produce backdrops for stop-motion animations and claymations using green screen technologies (see Chapter 11).

MOVING FULL STEAM AHEAD...

This chapter described the lifelong artistic pursuits of Alma Thomas and how they inspired her creative ideas, sense of beauty, advocacy practices, and innovations as an artist and educator. We learned about solar eclipses and sun safety. We can utilize Thomas's *Space Series* and marionettes to teach students about engineering star-studded marionette productions and creating stop motion animations and claymations. In the next chapter, we will continue to study the artistic behavior of idea development as we learn about Deborah Butterfield and her sculpted horses.

References

Chen, I. M., Tay, R., Xing, S., & Yeo, S. H. (2004). Marionette: From traditional manipulation to robotic manipulation. In M. Ceccarelli (Ed.), *International symposium on history of machines and mechanisms* (pp. 119–133). Springer.

Feman, S. (2021). The education of Miss Alma Thomas. In S. Feman, & J. F. Walz (Eds.), *Alma W. Thomas: Everything is beautiful* (pp. 108–115). Yale University Press.

Munro, E. (1979, April 15). The late spring time of Alma Thomas. *Washington Post Magazine.* https://www.washingtonpost.com/archive/lifestyle/magazine/1979/04/15/the-late-spring-time-of-alma-thomas/f205cbf7-3483-4cc4-8a52-7f5eacda7925/

Smithsonian Institution Archives of American Art. (2019, August 13). *Autobiographical writings by Alma Thomas, circa 1960s–circa 1970s.* https://edan.si.edu/transcription/pdf_files/17790.pdf

Walz, J. F. (2021). Vibratile offering: Alma Thomas's moving pictures. In S. Feman, & J. F. Walz (Eds.), *Alma W. Thomas: Everything is beautiful* (pp. 75–91). Yale University Press.

Chapter 6

Deborah Butterfield

Horse Power Leading the Way

FIGURE 6.1 Deborah Butterfield, *Three Sorrows,* 2016 cast bronze, wood, plastic, and wire. Horse: 81.25 × 100.75 × 40 in. (206.4 × 255.9 × 101.6 cm).
Source: L. A. Louver. © 2021 Deborah Butterfield/Licensed by VAGA at Artists Rights Society (ARS), NY.

Deborah Butterfield has created larger-than-life sculpted horses that are widely collected and displayed in museums. Each horse is a unique being. Butterfield's fluency of forms and use of materials are the results of her artistic skills combined with her thorough knowledge, understanding, and care for horses. She carefully selects found objects and arranges them into exact positions to present her horses' vitalities. The found objects' flowing contour lines characterize her horses' supportive musculoskeletal systems and distinct dispositions.

Butterfield departed from presenting horses as impressive mounts symbolizing the status of elite rulers on heroic war

horses (Louver, 2012). Her horses are gentle and tranquil, yet powerful. When fewer women were represented in art history books and exhibitions, Butterfield designed a horse lying down in an exhibition space as an autobiographical analogy for her strength to face art critics and manage the harshest criticism without the need to act defensively—as lying down is a symbol of full relaxation for horses that can sleep while standing (Copeland, 2020).

Butterfield casts her sculpted horses' bodies in bronze and adds patina to their surfaces to return the appearance of natural wood. She explained: "I have used different materials in my work to invoke

DOI: 10.4324/9781003183693-8

different states of being, both physical and mental" (Butterfield, 2019, 3rd para). Her sculptural materials include burnt wood and debris resulting from human-made and natural disasters. They serve as powerful narratives that bring awareness to issues—including climate change. Her installation *Three Sorrows* (Figure 6.1) centers on a horse's figure that Butterfield constructed using cast bronze and debris from the Tohoku tsunami. A large blue plastic fishing drum forms the horse's core. The installation's themes "three sorrows: quake, tsunami, and meltdown" were inspired by Gretel Ehrlich's book *Facing the Wave* that recounts survivors' stories from the 2011 Tohoku earthquake and tsunami and the resulting Fukushima nuclear disaster. Fragmented fishing nets, buoys, plastic bottles, and branches surround Butterfield's horse and create a landscape of debris.

Butterfield recognizes her horses' strength and compares them to the power of rogue waves—as their natural behaviors can harm people (Louver, 2017). Viewers can witness the impacts of the ocean's powerful force by looking closely at *Three Sorrows* horse's plastic fishing drum, which has been ripped, discolored, and distorted. Its deformations identify the many battles it endured on its journey. Like rogue waves and powerful tsunamis, people must keep their eyes on the horses and understand their thoughts and actions. Describing *Three Sorrows*, Butterfield explained: "It's telling us what we have done to the environment" (Louver, 2012, 3:48); yet, she believes that not all people are listening to the horse's wisdom. In addition to their roles in educating society, Butterfield's horses, such as *Monekana* (Figure 6.2), are gentle creatures that make people feel calm and happy.

Given what we have learned about Butterfield and her horse sculptures, *Teaching and Learning in the STEAM Artist's Studio 6.1* invites students to create a sculpture that teaches about positive change. We will link the students' studies on Butterfield with the *STEAM Amplifiers'* instruction on plate tectonics (including earthquakes, tsunamis, and volcanos) and the impacts of plastics and acid rain on the environment.

Teaching and Learning in the STEAM Artist's Studio 6.1

Introduce students to Deborah Butterfield, the meaning of her sculpted horses, and the significance of the materials she selects to create them. Then, have students identify an animal to sculpt as a symbol to represent positive change.

Essential/Guiding Questions

1. How did Butterfield sculpt horses as symbols to lead the way for people to make better choices?
2. How did Butterfield's idea to use ocean debris add meaning to *Three Sorrows*? Would the meaning of *Three Sorrows* have changed if Butterfield had cast all of its parts as she did with *Monekana*?

Daily Learning Targets

As an artist, I can sculpt an animal in a stance that serves as a symbol that leads the way in making a positive change.

- I can research an animal and integrate the qualities that I learned about the animal in my sculpture.
- I can construct an armature (if needed) by arranging materials, such as wire and aluminum foil, to form a balanced design.
- I can create my animal using sculpting materials.
- I can integrate found objects and/or recycled materials into my design.

National Core Arts Anchor Standards NVAS 2, 6, 9, and 11. www.nationalartsstandards.org

Teaching for Students' Development

PK-12: (A) Provide resources to assist students in researching their chosen animals. Explain how artists design animals as symbols for positive changes. (B) Present age-appropriate videos on plate tectonics, plastics, recycling, and acid rain and their connections to human and animal life.

Early childhood: Young children learn from exploratory acts. Have students act out the movements of horses and other animals to understand their physical forms. Read children's books that use animal characters that teach about leading the way to positive changes to spark students' ideas for character development. Demonstrate how to model animal forms with pliable materials like soft clay and soft wire and then attach found objects to their forms.

Middle childhood: Students want to share their perceptions. Have students compare different animal characters from books, cartoons, and toys and explain how they feel the characters encourage people to take positive actions. Demonstrate how to manipulate found objects and repurpose them to form animal designs.

Early adolescence: Middle school students can present their perspectives supported by contextual information. Have students participate in a scavenger hunt to locate animal mascots and evaluate the contextual meanings of their designs' effectiveness in invoking people's responses. Challenge students to form their animal designs using at least 50% repurposed plastics or found objects.

Adolescence: High school students can use contextual evidence to explain how plastics negatively impact the environment and the health of living beings. Referencing artists' works, like Butterfield's, they can describe how repurposing plastics into art can minimize plastic waste in oceans and landfills. Challenge students to form their animal designs using at least 60% repurposed plastics.

FIGURE 6.2 Deborah Butterfield, *Monekana*, 2001, bronze, 96 × 129 ½ × 63 ½ in. (243.8 × 328.9 × 161.3 cm).

Source: Smithsonian American Art Museum. © Deborah Butterfield.

STEAM AMPLIFIERS CHOICE #1—UNDERSTANDING EARTHQUAKES

Referencing Butterfield's *Three Sorrows*, explain to students that an **earthquake** is the rapid shaking and shifting of the **lithosphere** (the top layer of the earth's surface) that causes rock to break or slip along **fault lines**. The lithosphere is subdivided into 12 major landmasses called **tectonic plates**. The tectonic plates lock together like puzzle pieces. Due to their lighter weight, they float on the earth's mantle (molten rock), which is heavier. Their slow movement is termed the **continental drift**. When two tectonic plates interact through **compression** (moving together), **tension** (moving apart), and **shearing** (scraping), they cause friction, vibrations, and stress. These powerful forces break rock and reshape the lithosphere causing earthquakes, volcanos, and tsunamis.

The **hypocenter** is the location in the earth's crust where the earthquake initiates. The **epicenter** is the point on the earth's surface located directly above the hypocenter and is usually where the greatest earthquake destruction occurs. When an earthquake's epicenter is located at sea it can produce a tsunami (see Chapter 7), like the Tohoku tsunami. Earthquakes produce **seismic shock waves** that penetrate the earth's interior and vibrate its surface. Seismologists record seismic waves using an instrument called the **seismograph** that measures an earthquake's **slip** (displacement along a fault), **magnitude** (energy release), and length. The magnitude is measured at seismic detection stations across the planet using a universal **Moment Magnitude Scale** that provides the best size calculations of large earthquakes. The 2011 Tohoku earthquake measured at M_W 9.0. (Learn more about earthquakes on the companion website.)

Given their studies on earthquakes, students can develop an information campaign that teaches about earthquakes and earthquake safety. As an extension activity, they can study how built environment specialists combine their knowledge of science, engineering, and design to produce earthquake-resistant buildings, roads, and bridges.

STEAM AMPLIFIERS CHOICE #2—VOLCANOLOGY

Two days after the Tohoku earthquake and tsunami, a powerful volcano eruption occurred at Shinmoedake—500 miles away. **Volcanology** is the study of **volcanos**, which are formed when the earth's core radiates heat as hot as the sun into the earth's next layer, the **mantle**, and melts molten rock, called **magma**. The magma chamber rises upward to the earth's surface when the layers are stressed and/or thinned and trapped gasses build

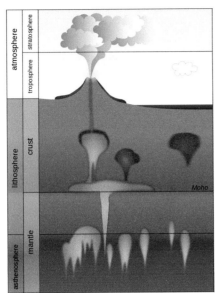

FIGURE 6.3 This illustration shows how magma forms in the earth's mantle and rises to the surface to produce a volcano eruption. *Source: USGS. Public Domain.*

pressure (see Figure 6.3). Magma that rises through the earth's crust and escapes through fractures and vents produces volcanic eruptions. Magma that reaches the air is called **lava**.

Analyzing data from the Shinmoedake eruption and other regional volcanos, scientists determined that the Tohoku earthquake may have caused Shinmoedake's increased seismic activity (Wang et al., 2011). Like volcanologists, students can learn how to classify volcanos—including the **cinder cone, composite volcano (stratovolcano), caldera (super volcano),** and **shield volcano**—by their shape, size, the materials that form them, and types of eruptions. (See information on the companion website.) Given examples of the types of volcanos and their properties, students can apply their knowledge to create sketches and sculpted models of volcanos. They can participate in a scavenger hunt to identify different types of

volcanos in art, such as Hokusai's *Under the Wave off Kanagawa* that shows Mt. Fuji (see Chapter 7).

STEAM AMPLIFIERS CHOICE #3—MEASURING THE IMPACTS OF ACID RAIN

Years after its creation, Butterfield examined *Monekana* (Figure 6.2) inside the Smithsonian American Art Museum (2017) and noticed that its patina has not been damaged by climate factors, especially acid rain, like sculptures exhibited outdoors. **Acid rain** is a pollutant present in precipitation that includes rain, snow, sleet, and fog. It is formed when the compounds sulfur dioxide (SO_2) and nitrogen oxide (NO_x) are released into the air when emissions from power plants (coal, oil, and natural gas), factories, and cars mix with water and oxygen. This harmful mixture is carried by the

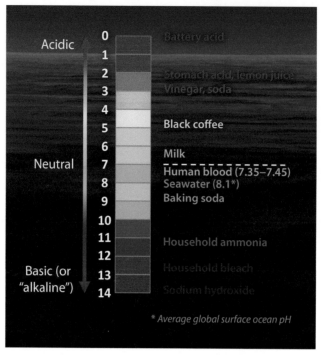

FIGURE 6.4 The pH scale ranges from 0 to 14. With each number increase, the amount of acid is 10 times greater.
Source: NOAA's PMEL Carbon Program.

wind and can travel long distances. The stronger the acid content, the greater the damage. It causes freshwater streams and lakes to become so toxic that they can no longer support life. It destroys whole forests and depletes the soil of nutrients necessary for growth. As noted by Butterfield, acid rain also damages art in the built environment.

Scientists measure acidity on a pH scale that ranges from 0 to 14. Acid rain typically measures at 4.0 but can reach much lower in extreme conditions. Students can use litmus paper to conduct tests to measure acid and base levels (see Figure 6.4's pH scale). They can identify ways to reduce acid rain by switching to renewable energies—including solar and wind (see Chapter 12); strategies to drive less, such as bike riding, using public transportation (see Chapter 14), and carpooling; and, reducing energy in their homes. (Learn more about acid rain on this book's companion website.)

STEAM AMPLIFIERS CHOICE #4—PLASTIC MARINE DEBRIS

Like acid rain, plastics cause substantial harm to the environment (Figure 6.5). **Plastic** is formed from natural organic or synthetic polymers, which are long chains of molecules made up of smaller molecules. Plastic abounds in our daily lives as it is used in packaging, products, and more. Most plastics are made with fossil fuels, such as petroleum (crude oil), natural gas, and coal. While people recognize large plastic debris called **macroplastics**, like the drum in Butterfield's horse, the

FIGURE 6.5 Deborah Butterfield's *Three Sorrows* is made with plastic marine debris.
Source: L. A. Louver. © 2021 Deborah Butterfield/ Licensed by VAGA at Artists Rights Society (ARS), NY.

ocean is also filled with microscopic plastic particles called **microplastics** that measure less than 5 mm. Plastic is particularly harmful to the environment due to its production practices and slow decomposition rates. Sea birds and marine animals are harmed and killed by ingesting and/or becoming entangled in plastic. Despite its harmful impacts on the environment, the fossil fuel industry continues to increase its production of plastics, including single-use plastics (Niranjan, 2020).

By 2025, with increased plastic production, it is estimated that humans will add over 17.5 million metric tons of plastic to the oceans annually (Jambeck et al., 2015). Massive garbage patches have formed in our oceans due to winds and ocean **gyres** (rotating currents) that amass plastic debris together. Tsunami debris adds more plastic to the existing masses already in the ocean. Their enormous scale and continuous motions make garbage patches difficult to eliminate.

Building on their studies of Butterfield's *Three Sorrows*, students will learn how to reduce, reuse, recycle, and properly dispose of plastics to cause less harm to the oceans and their communities. Resources, such as the Marine Debris Toolkit for Educators (Nally et al., 2017), offer instructional videos, lesson plans, and scientific investigations including data collection and data analysis for student advocacy campaigns.

MOVING FULL STEAM AHEAD...

This chapter described how Deborah Butterfield has applied her creative ideas to sculpt graceful horses that bring awareness to contemporary issues including the environment and the representation of female artists in art history books and art exhibitions. It completes Part II of this book that focuses on the artistic behavior of idea development. The chapter's *STEAM Amplifiers* presented contextual information about earthquakes, volcanos, acid rain, and plastic marine debris. In the next section of this book, Part III, we will explore the artistic behavior of observation. Part III begins with Katsushika Hokusai and his infamous artwork *Under the Wave off Kanagawa*, also known as *The Great Wave*.

References

Butterfield, D. (2019). Deborah Butterfield: Billings. https://www.tinworksart.org/deborah-butterfield

Copeland, C. (2020, November 14) The horse as witness and metaphor: A chat with Deborah Butterfield. *Glasstire.* https://glasstire.com/2020/11/14/ the-horse-as-witness-and-metaphor-a-chat-with-deborah-butterfield/

Jambeck, J., Andrady, A., Geyer, R., Narayan, R., Perryman, M., Siegler, T., Wilcox, C., & Lavender Law, K. (2015). Plastic waste inputs from land into the ocean. *Science, 347*(6223), 768–771. doi: 10.1126/science.1260352.

Louver, L. A. (2012, November 30). *Deborah Butterfield at L.A. Louver (2012)* [Video]. https://www.youtube.com/watch?v=1_kg_YgEzNA

Louver., L. A. (2017, December 18). *Deborah Butterfield: Three Sorrows.* [Video]. https://www.youtube.com/watch?v=mXS-iuXv1rs

Nally, A., Lippiatt, S., Nachbar, S., & Pollack, N. (2017). *Marine debris toolkit for educators.* NOAA Marine Debris Program. https://marinedebris.noaa.gov/sites/default/files/publications-files/MarineDebrisMonitoring ToolkitForEducators.pdf

Niranjan, A. (2020, March 26). Oil companies pivot to plastics to stave off losses from fuel demand. *Deutsche Welle.* https://p.dw.com/p/3Zghx

Smithsonian American Art Museum. (2017). *Monekana.* https://americanart.si.edu/artwork/monekana-71406

Wang, F., Shen, Z., Wang, Y., & Want, M. (2011). Influence of the March 11, 2011 Mw 9.0 Tohokuoki earthquake on regional volcanic activities. *Chinese Science Bulletin, 56*(20), pp. 2077–2081. doi: 10.1007/s11434-011-4523-y.

PART III

Artists' Lessons to Thrive! Observation

Chapter 7

Katsushika Hokusai

Capturing a Great Wave

FIGURE 7.1 Katsushika Hokusai, *Under the Wave off Kanagawa*, also known as *The Great Wave*, from the series *Thirty-six Views of Mount Fuji*, ca. 1830–32. Woodblock print; ink and color on paper.
Source: www.metmuseum.org. (CC0 1.0).

Katsushika Hokusai's infamous print *Under the Wave off Kanagawa*, nicknamed *The Great Wave*, captures a dramatic natural event (Figure 7.1). A larger-than-life wave dominates the artwork's composition and serves as its focal point. Hokusai presented the wave at eye level to add to its sensational effects. The boats and humans feel insignificant in comparison—as does Mount Fuji, which normally dominates the surrounding landscape. Several droplets spray outward from the wave into the atmosphere and appear to sprinkle delicate snowflakes on Mount Fuji. Next to the droplets, the wave's foaming crest reveals its full power with the appearance of jagged fingers reaching forcefully downward toward three oshiokuri boats populated with fishermen. The fishermen hunker down clutching their oars and brace for impact. Under calmer conditions, they would be standing upright rowing their fast cargo ships to collect fish and other goods for transport.

This famous artwork is an **ukiyo-e** print—meaning an artwork that presents views of the floating world, an analogy for depictions of Japan's entertainment forms, everyday events, and beautiful landscapes—mass produced for people's

DOI: 10.4324/9781003183693-10

enjoyment. *Under the Wave off Kanagawa* belongs to Hokusai's series titled *Thirty-Six Views of Mt. Fuji*. Hokusai illustrated Japan's highest mountain from different perspectives and under diverse weather conditions. He skillfully captured details and nuances to render the series' landscapes, architectural structures, vessels, animals, and people.

Since the 1960s, *Under the Wave off Kanagawa* has been referred to as a **tsunami** due to its massive size and the fear it evokes (see Figure 7.2). Tsunamis occur when large amounts of energy are suddenly displaced by earthquakes, underground volcano eruptions, and submarine landslides (see Chapter 6). The underwater

energy and friction offset the normal equilibrium. Water shifts vertically and causes the imbalances that form tsunamis. As the deep-water mass reaches toward the shore and hits shallow waters, **wave shoaling** occurs—meaning the velocity decreases and the wave crests can reach heights over 100 feet (30 m), causing devastating harm to life and structures on shore.

The Japanese name tsunami means harbor wave because fishermen would first notice tsunamis and their devastation upon returning to shore. Tsunamis appear inconspicuous in deep waters because they have long and shallow forms. Hokusai's fishermen in *Under the Wave off Kanagawa* are fully aware of the menacing wave. With this knowledge, scholars Cartwright and Nakamura (2009) hypothesized that *Under the Wave off Kanagawa* was a storm wave rather than a tsunami. Given their close examinations of the artwork and actual landscape, historical data, and mathematical and scientific reasoning skills, they determined that the great wave was more likely a **rogue wave**—one that is large in size, produced by a storm, appears suddenly, and can move in directions different from surrounding waves. Cartwright and Nakamura compared the historical characteristics of tsunamis that entered the artwork's location—present-day Tokyo Bay—with the height of Hokusai's wave and the boat lengths measuring 39–49 feet (12–15 m). They determined the 32+ foot (10+ m) wave was about twice as large as typical 18 foot (5.6 m) tsunamis that enter the bay. The bay's inlet is too narrow to produce the gigantic tsunami waves that hit the nearby Pacific shoreline.

FIGURE 7.2 Katsushika Hokusai's *Under the Wave off Kanagawa* has been incorrectly identified as a tsunami on warning signs and brochures including this 1965 Coast and Geodetic Survey cover.

Source: NOAA. Public Domain.

Hokusai's artworks inspire feelings of awe and provide a wealth of visual data for people to make reasoned correlations that link his art with nature's occurrences and scientific understandings. He created *Thirty-Six Views of Mt. Fuji* in his 70s—a time in life when he believed that he truly understood drawing's structures. Describing himself as "mad about drawing" (Thomas, 2015, p. 9), the artist who began drawing at age six spent decades refining his drawing skills by creating observational drawings and paying keen attention to details. These skills assisted him in convincingly drawing what he saw and representing events based on other people's accounts—as is most likely the case with *Under the Wave off Kanagawa*.

To teach *Teaching and Learning in the STEAM Artist's Studio 7.1*, we will apply what we have learned about Hokusai and demonstrate how to make an accordion book (Figure 7.3). We can enhance our teaching with content from its *STEAM Amplifiers* that teach about waves, art criticism, Gyotaku printing, and severe weather conditions.

FIGURE 7.3 Teacher Sara Nixon presents her accordion book. She created its pockets by folding the bottom third of the paper upward and then making the accordion folds.
Source: Photo: Pamela McColly.

Teaching and Learning in the STEAM Artist's Studio 7.1

Introduce Katsushika Hokusai and ukiyo-e prints to students. Discuss the characteristics of waves and severe weather conditions. Ask students to make correlations to what they see in *Under the Wave off Kanagawa*. Demonstrate the process of making an accordion book that includes wave-inspired subject matter, one or more printmaking techniques, and an original haiku. Explain that the **haiku** originates from Japan and is a verse that does not rhyme. It traditionally describes nature and the seasons. The haiku is three lines long with a 5-7-5-syllable structure.

Essential/Guiding Questions

1. Hokusai was an avid drawer who included subtle details in his art. What noticeable details do you see in *Under the Wave off Kanagawa*? Why are they important?
2. How can paying attention to details benefit people in everyday life? Identify a time in your life in which you paid attention to details and how it benefited you.

Daily Learning Targets

As an artist, I can create an accordion book with a wave-inspired theme.

- I can design my accordion book by completing its front and back cover pages, interior pages, and backside pages.
- I can incorporate fine details into my designs and make revisions based on my observations.
- I can integrate at least one printmaking technique in my design.

I can write an original haiku inspired by wave subject matter.

- I can follow the 5-7-5-syllable haiku structure. (The first line is five syllables; the second line is seven syllables; the third line is five syllables.)
- I can unify my book's design and haiku poem so that they belong together.

National Core Arts Anchor Standards NVAS 3, 5, 9, and 11.
www.nationalartsstandards.org

Teaching for Students' Development

PK-12: (A) Teach students how to write a haiku using a wave as its inspiration. (B) Demonstrate the process of creating a haiku accordion book. Have students brainstorm ways to add details to their art.

Early childhood: Young children can explain how they are making their art. Facilitate students in learning how to create a haiku collaboratively with teacher guidance. Monitor students who are working and talk to them about their progress. Have students participate in a class critique to describe their completed artwork and its haiku.

Middle childhood: Students communicate meaning by adding details to their art. Check the students' construction of a haiku using the 5-7-5 syllable pattern. Discuss the importance of adding details to artworks to communicate information. Monitor the class and talk to them about ways to incorporate details to connect their book's visual images with the haiku they developed. During a final critique, ask students to describe how details enhanced their artworks' meanings.

Early adolescence: Middle school students can describe how prominent features in their artworks communicate ideas. Ask students to identify the key elements that make their book original and how their book's design communicates the haiku's meaning.

Adolescence: High school students can identify plans for making revisions to their art. Have students participate in a formative art critique to describe their plans to make necessary revisions to unify their book's design with their haiku. During a summative critique, ask students to identify how their revisions improved their final artworks.

FIGURE 7.4 Students at Fire Island National Seashore interpret their observations of ocean waves using art media. (cropped photograph)

Source: NPS National Park Service Northeast Region. Flickr, Public Domain Mark 1.0.

STEAM AMPLIFIERS CHOICE #1—UNDERSTANDING WAVES

Waves are produced by the energy flows that cause water to rise and fall. Under normal conditions, waves are formed by winds and tides impacted by gravitational pulls. Scientists use mathematical formulas to measure the energy and sizes of waves, as was the case in determining that Hokusai's great wave was most likely a rogue wave. When studying *Under the Wave off Kanagawa*, students benefit from learning waves' properties (see Figures 7.4 and 7.5). For example, a **crest** is a wave's highest point. The **trough** identifies a wave's lowest point. **Amplitude** identifies the greatest distance of displacement—either the crest's high point or the trough's low point—from a wave's normal rested position. The **wavelength** marks the distance between two crests. The time it takes for a wave to travel from one point to the next is called a **wave period**. Scientists measure a wave's **frequency** by selecting a point and counting the number of wave crests per second. Given their studies on waves, students can collect artworks with waves as their subject matter and analyze the waves' properties. They can record their findings through writing and sketching in their journals.

STEAM AMPLIFIERS CHOICE #2—INTERPRETING *UNDER THE WAVE OFF KANAGAWA*

Cartwright and Nakamura (2009) hypothesized that Hokusai's wave was a storm wave rather than a tsunami. As part of their investigation, they carefully examined *Under the Wave off Kanagawa*.

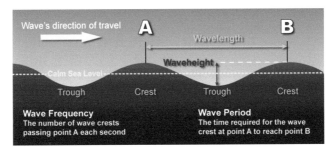

FIGURE 7.5 Anatomy of a wave chart.
Source: NOAA. Public Domain.

They understood that although Hokusai simplified areas of his composition and made artistic changes, he aimed to provide realistic impressions of the environments he illustrated. Similar to scientific investigations, art criticism calls upon viewers to look closely at artworks. Using Anderson's (1997) art criticism model, the following art criticism inquiry questions can assist students in noticing details, analyzing meanings, and forming educated judgments about *Under the Wave off Kanagawa*.

- What are the first things you think and feel when looking at Hokusai's *Under the Wave off Kanagawa*?
- How would you describe *Under the Wave off Kanagawa* to someone who has never seen it?
- What is *Under the Wave off Kanagawa's* focal point? What makes you look there? Why do you think that Hokusai chose to emphasize that area?
- How did Hokusai's technical observational drawing skills and attention to details assist him in capturing the look and feel of *Under the Wave off Kanagawa*?
- What would you be thinking if you were a passenger on one of the oshiokuri boats?
- What can *Under the Wave off Kanagawa* teach us about waves?
- Based on your descriptions and interpretations, is *Under the Wave off Kanagawa* an important artwork? Explain your answer.

After participating in the art criticism discussion, students can conduct an Internet search to listen to a performance of Claude Debussy's musical composition *La Mer*, which was inspired by Hokusai's *Under the Wave off Kanagawa*. They can compare their impressions about the feelings that Hokusai's and Debussy's creative works evoke about waves.

STEAM AMPLIFIERS CHOICE #3—GYOTAKU FISH PRINTING

During the Edo Period (17th–19th centuries) when Hokusai produced his Ukiyo-e prints, Japanese fishermen would tell great accounts of the fish they caught at sea. To add validity to their fish tales, they recorded their catches' actual sizes by creating gyotaku prints. In Japanese, *gyo* means fish and *taku* means impression. The fishermen applied natural sumi ink made from pine soot directly to the cleaned fish they caught and transferred their impressions of the fish to **washi** paper. As part of a unit of study, students will learn the parts of a fish and ways to protect natural fish stocks. They can study sustainable fishing practices that avoid overfishing and research sustainable fish farming that bans antibiotics, hormones, and other additives. To conclude their studies, students can create gyotaku prints using rubber gyotaku fish replicas (Figure 7.6) and develop advocacy campaigns that include informative stories and artworks illustrating what they have learned about sustainable fishing and farming.

STEAM AMPLIFIERS CHOICE #4—SEVERE WEATHER CONDITIONS

Meteorology is the scientific study of the atmosphere to understand climate and weather conditions and make

forecasts. Severe weather is a meteorological topic of particular interest due to the harm and damage it can cause. Examples include drought, flooding, hail, high winds, thunderstorms, tornados, hurricanes/typhoons, and wildfires. Students will investigate the different types of severe weather and their effects around the globe (Figures 7.7 and 7.8). They will compare and contrast normal weather conditions in their own communities with severe weather conditions in past and present times. If available, they can interview and collaborate with meteorologists and/or weather specialists to conduct their research. Students will document their findings and prepare public service announcements to teach what they have learned.

FIGURE 7.7 Katsushika Hokusai, Ejiri in Suruga Province (Sunshū Ejiri), from the series Thirty-six Views of Mount Fuji (Fugaku sanjūrokkei), from the series *Thirty-six Views of Mount Fuji*, ca. 1830–32. Woodblock print; ink and color on paper.
Source: www.metmuseum.org. (CC0 1.0).

MOVING FULL STEAM AHEAD...

Katsushika Hokusai's *Under the Wave off Kanagawa* and the work of Cartwright and Nakamura brought to our attention the importance of observation, paying attention to details, collecting data, and using analysis in STEAM. In the next chapter, we will study Claude Monet, who was greatly inspired by Hokusai and other Japanese ukiyo-e printmakers.

FIGURE 7.8 Dark thunderstorm clouds dominate the landscape at St. Mark's lighthouse.
Source: © Richard Sickler.

Monet's knowledge of Japanese art and horticulture, combined with his observation skills, influenced his creation of his infamous water garden at Giverny and the many plein-air (outdoor) paintings he created there.

References

Anderson, T. (1997). A model for art criticism: Talking with kids about art. *School Arts, 97*(1), 21–24.

Cartwright, J., & Nakamura, H. (2009, February 25). What kind of a wave is Hokusai's Great Wave Off Kanagawa? *Notes and Records of the Royal Society, 63*(2), 119–135 https://doi.org/10.1098/rsnr.2007.0039

Thomas, S. E. (2015). *Hokusai.* MFA Publications.

Chapter 8

Claude Monet

Cultivating Artistic Vision

FIGURE 8.1 Claude Monet, *Water Lily Pond*, 1900. Oil on canvas, 89.8 × 101 cm (35 3/8 × 39 3/4 in.).
Source: Art Institute of Chicago. (CC0) Public Domain.

In Claude Monet's water garden in Giverny, France, tall grasses sway in the breeze as branches of weeping willows cascade gracefully into a pond below that bustles with colorful water lilies, frogs ribbiting, native carp splashing, and birds singing. The scents of fresh flowers fill the air. Claude Monet first imagined these serene and sensual water garden qualities and brought them to life when he was able to purchase the property he was renting and its adjoining land. To design the water garden, Monet combined his knowledge of art and **horticulture**—a type of agriculture that focuses on the scientific and aesthetic study of plants, flowers, and trees. Monet's choice of water lilies stemmed from seeing horticulturalist Joseph Bory Latour-Marliac's invention of hardy hybrid water lilies that blended indigenous white French water lilies with colorful foreign ones (Van Dyke, 2019). Monet also referred to Japanese art for his garden's design. He had an extensive collection of Japanese ukiyo-e woodblock prints (see Chapter 7) that illustrated stunning Japanese landscapes

DOI: 10.4324/9781003183693-11

with attractive footbridges. The artist obtained permits to divert stream water that branched off the Epte River to supply his water garden with its diversified plant life including native and Japanese plants (Wildenstein, 1978). The permits stipulated that the stream water must remain free-flowing without sluices (gates) and that the garden would not interfere with the health of the natural ecosystem.

Monet's interest in art and gardening began in childhood and continued throughout his life. He read about horticulture, met with expert gardeners, and collected plants from distant lands. Monet was attracted to Giverny's landscapes as sources for his **plein-air**—open-air paintings. As he aged, he wanted to remain at home and paint his gardens (National Gallery of Victoria, 2013). Water lilies became his main painting subject beginning in the late 1890s. Like his earlier Impressionist paintings, Monet studied how the times of day and the seasons changed the lights and colors of his garden. *Water Lily Pond* from 1900 (Figure 8.1) presents a view of Monet's largest bridge arching across his garden's pond. The pond's surface is densely speckled with water lilies. Plant life abounds. As his style evolved, some of Monet's compositions focused primarily on the pond—eliminating the surrounding sky and landscape. To acknowledge their existence, he painted their reflections on the water's surface (Figure 8.2).

In his 60s, Monet began to experience profound vision loss. He was diagnosed with age-related bilateral cataracts in 1912 (Gruener, 2015). He could no longer see colors as he had before.

FIGURE 8.2 Claude Monet, *Water Lilies*, 1906. Oil on canvas, 89.9 × 94.1 cm (35 3/8 × 37 1/16 in.).
Source: Art Institute of Chicago. (CC0) Public Domain.

Colors looked dull yellow and brown. Glaring sunlight was also disturbing to his eyes. These changes were extremely challenging for the artists whose artistic vision focused on presenting colors' subtle changes over time. By 1914–15 Monet noticed that his painting palette had become darker. Colors he knew before looked muddy. He had difficulty distinguishing colors. To compensate, he read paint labels to know what colors they were and planned their arrangement on his palette. He also relied on his artistic visions from past experiences to guide and correct colors lost to his diminished sight. Analyzing Monet's vision loss based on the artist's medical records and written accounts, Dr. Michael Marmor (2006), a contemporary ophthalmologist, described how Monet's vision declined. In 1912, Monet's vision was probably 20/50 on an eye chart that measures visual acuity. Ten years later, his best-functioning eye was measured at 20/200. Marmor

FIGURE 8.3 Claude Monet, *Water Lily Pond*, 1917/19. Oil on canvas, 130.2 × 201.9 cm (51 1/2 × 79 1/2 in.).

Source: Art Institute of Chicago. CC0 Public Domain.

FIGURE 8.4 Claude Monet, *The Japanese Bridge*, 1923–25. Oil on canvas, 35 × 45 3/4 in. (88.9 × 116.21 cm).

Source: Minneapolis Institute of Art. Public Domain.

modeled what Monet's vision probably looked like by blurring and darkening color photographs of Monet's paintings and water garden to make clear comparisons with Monet's paintings that contained fewer details and had a darker color palette. For example, his 1917/19 painting *Water Lily Pond* (Figure 8.3) has a darker hue than his previous pond scenes. His 1923/25 painting *The Japanese Bridge* (Figure 8.4) includes warmer colors and coarser brushstrokes than his previous pond landscapes.

After two cataract surgeries and the use of specialized glasses, Monet's vision improved. Monet was then able to paint with a more naturalistic and detailed color palette.

Working with the artistic behavior of observation, we will discuss the relevance of Monet's observations when developing his water garden and paintings at Giverny to teach *Teaching and Learning in the STEAM Artist's Studio 8.1*. We will reinforce the importance of observation when

Teaching and Learning in the STEAM Artist's Studio 8.1

Introduce students to Claude Monet's water lily paintings, their varying qualities, and the meanings of artistic vision. Have students identify desirable places on their school campus and/or the broader community to produce plein-air artworks. After identifying their locations, the class can sketch, paint, and take photographs in the open air to create a two- or three-dimensional artwork, such as a diorama that includes built environment structures. Students can utilize binoculars and camera lenses to enhance their observations and identify environmental features such as water sources, built environment structures, and plant and animal life.

Essential/Guiding Questions

1. What does it mean to have an artistic vision? How did Monet utilize his understandings of art and horticulture to present his artistic visions to the world?
2. In your opinion, why was it important for Monet to continue painting and make accommodations as his vision diminished?

Daily Learning Targets

As an artist, I can create a plein-air artwork inspired by Monet's water garden.

- I can create my artwork in two- or three-dimensions.
- I can select the materials of my choice.
- I can integrate a built environment feature into my design if I choose to.
- I can produce a unified design.

National Core Arts Anchor Standards NVAS 2, 6, 8, and 10.
www.nationalartsstandards.org

Teaching for Students' Development

PK-12: (A) Discuss the importance of observation in STEAM and how careful observations enable STEAM professionals to make discoveries. (B) Brainstorm how looking closely assists artists in adding important visual details to their art and communicating meaning.

Early childhood: Young children are learning how to observe their environment and can utilize what they see as inspirations for creating art. Use this practice to build students' observational skills. Their plein-air artworks will look more expressive than realistic because their manipulative skills are still developing.

Middle childhood: Students can point to evidence in artworks to identify where they were created. Ask students to incorporate recognizable features that represent their plein-air artworks' locations as clues to inform others.

Early adolescence: Middle school students can identify how STEAM professionals use observational skills to form understandings. During a class critique, have students discuss how their development of plein-air artworks deepened their understandings of their chosen locations.

Adolescence: High school students can participate in art inquiry tasks to identify artists' varied reasons for using observational skills to produce art. After completing their plein-air artworks, students can write an artist statement that describes the purposeful role of observation in their work.

FIGURE 8.5 A student uses observational drawing skills to study water lilies at Kenilworth Aquatic Gardens.
Source: National Park Service. Flickr, (CC by 2.0).

creating plein-air artworks (Figure 8.5). The *STEAM Amplifiers* describe protecting our watersheds; building bridges; ophthalmology, optometry, and artistic vision; and include a scavenger hunt.

STEAM AMPLIFIERS CHOICE #1—PROTECTING OUR WATERSHEDS

Local residents in Giverny were concerned about maintaining the quality of the local water that they relied on and felt hesitant when Monet proposed diverting water to nourish his garden from the Ru stream that branched off of the Epte River (Wildenstein, 1978). They believed that using the water for the garden with its non-native plants could be harmful. Monet obtained the necessary permits to use the water given the condition that the natural ecosystem would not be harmed. Like Giverny's residents in Monet's time, people in contemporary society want access to clean, healthy water (see Chapter 9).

A **watershed** is a dividing land area or ridge where rainwater and snowmelt drain into a single water source. People

rely on healthy watersheds to preserve water quality, maintain the natural environment, and promote biodiversity. Students will learn that **surface-water** watersheds are located on the surfaces of land. They include rivers, streams, lakes, and wetlands. **Groundwater** watersheds receive water from higher points and drain to sources including underground rivers and aquifers. Students can study the local watershed(s) in their communities. They can reference the US Forest Service's (Potyondy & Geier, 2011) National Watershed Condition Team's three classifications that include Class 1 = Functioning Properly, Class 2 = Functioning at Risk, and Class 3 = Impaired Function. Ideally, all watersheds should be identified as Class 1 to support healthy ecosystems. We can introduce students to local, state, and national laws about preserving water quality and bring in environmental experts (as available) for students to study the factors that contribute to healthy watersheds and how human behaviors can positively and negatively impact watersheds. Students can also learn about the water cycle and the steps environmental engineers take to treat drinking water. Working in teams, students will disseminate the information they learned using visual and/or media arts resources.

STEAM AMPLIFIERS CHOICE #2—BUILDING BRIDGES

Monet was inspired by the Japanese footbridges he saw in u-kiyo-e prints and had similar models constructed because their functional designs added aesthetic beauty to his water garden. Students will learn about the different types of bridges (including beam, arch, and suspension) and their purposes. When inventorying bridges, students can identify obstacles that include bodies of water, railroad tracks, and streets. They will learn that engineers design bridges and rely on the forces of **compression** (pushing together) and **tension** (pulling apart) to stabilize their designs. Engineers identify bridges' intended functions, necessary materials, and costs. For example, Monet's bridges are arch bridges that could not support the same weight and quantity of vehicles and pedestrians as San Francisco's suspension *Golden Gate Bridge*. Engineers also analyze building foundations to ensure that the ground can support a bridge's weight. They plan for environmental stresses from natural forces such as heavy rains, high winds, and severe storms. Based on their studies, students can draw bridge designs and/or construct model bridges using set criteria—such as a footbridge for a garden or a bridge that would meet their community's needs (Figure 8.6). They will take into consideration bridge structures, usages, weather constraints, and the impacts of natural geology on supporting foundations.

FIGURE 8.6 Students constructed bridges and weighed how many pounds they could support during a one-week residence at the Oregon Institute of Technology. (cropped photograph)
Source: Oregon Department of Transportation. Flickr, (CC by 2.0).

STEAM AMPLIFIERS CHOICE #3—OPHTHALMOLOGY, OPTOMETRY, AND ARTISTIC VISION

Students will discuss vision science and study the characteristics of human eyes. Historical documents describe how Monet's vision improved with surgeries and specialized glasses. After an introduction to Monet and vision science, students can discuss ways to protect their eyes. Examples include practicing sun safety to minimize exposure to ultraviolet rays (see Chapter 5) and limiting screen time. Students might create illustrated guides that inform others how to keep their eyes safe. As part of their studies, students can learn about the professions of ophthalmologists and optometrists and how eye chart tests measure vision. They can also research the benefits of optical instruments that enhance vision including eyeglasses, magnifying glasses, binoculars, cameras, x-ray machines, telescopes, and microscopes (Figure 8.7). In addition to

FIGURE 8.7 Adolescents look through microscopes at Marsh-Billings-Rockefeller National Park during its Bio Blitz.
Source: National Park Service. Flickr, Public Domain Mark 1.0.

FIGURE 8.8 Tlingit, *Mosquito Mask*, before 1843, H. 4 1/3 × W. 6 3/4 in. (11 × 17.1 cm), Wood, paint, copper, shell, Native-tanned skin.
Source: www.metmuseum.org. (CC0 1.0).

Monet, students can study artists with low vision and blindness to identify how diverse artists make accommodations, use their senses, and work with assistive technologies to produce art.

STEAM AMPLIFIER CHOICE #4—WATER GARDEN SCAVENGER HUNT

Monet closely examined Japanese prints to identify the features that he wanted to include in his water garden design. Japanese maples, wisterias, and bamboos adorned Monet's garden. Native animals in his water garden include frogs, dragonflies, butterflies, bees, moorhens, herons, finches, carp, and pike. Students will participate in a scavenger hunt to locate artworks that include animals (Figures 8.8 and 8.9) and plants found in habitats that support water lilies, like Monet's water garden. They can use their collection for contextually-driven art inquiry tasks inspired by categorizing aesthetic works (see Chapter 13),

playing matching games, and identifying art historical data and genres.

MOVING FULL STEAM AHEAD...

This chapter taught about Monet and the importance of observation in creating his plain-air paintings at Giverny. It also addressed how Monet made accommodations to his painting techniques in

FIGURE 8.9 *Automation*, ca. 1820. Swiss. Gold, enamel, diamond, ruby. L. 6.2 cm (2 7/16 in.).
Source: www.metmuseum.org. (CC0 1.0).

response to his diminished eyesight. We will continue our studies of the artistic behavior of observation in the next chapter and learn about Grand Canyon National Park's Desert View and its transformation into an inter-tribal cultural heritage site.

References

Gruener, A. (2015). Out of hours: The effects of cataracts and cataract surgery on Claude Monet. *British Journal of General Practice, 65*(634), 254–255.

Marmor, M. F. (2006). Ophthalmology and art: Simulation of Monet's cataracts and Degas' retinal disease. *Arch Ophthalmol, 124*(12), 1764–1769. doi: 10.1001/archopht.124.12.1764.

National Gallery of Victoria. (2013). *A passion for gardening.* National Gallery of Victoria. https://web.archive.org/web/20131216221442/http://www.ngv.vic.gov.au/whats-on/exhibitions/exhibitions/monets-garden/explore/themes/a-passion-for-gardening

Potyondy, J. P., & Geier, T. W. (2011). *Watershed condition classification technical guide.* United States Department of Agriculture Forest Service. https://www.rosemonteis.us/sites/default/files/references/potyondy-geier-2011.pdf

Van Dyke, S. (2019, July 22). *Denver Botanical Garden's curator of aquatic collections discusses Monet's waterlilies.* Denver Art Museum. https://denverartmuseum.org/article/denver-botanic-gardens-curator-aquatic-collections-discusses-monets-waterlilies

Wildenstein, D. (1978). Monet's Giverny. *Metropolitan Museum of Art's Monet's years at Giverny: Beyond impressionism* (pp. 15–40). Harry N. Abrams.

Chapter 9

Desert View

Designing an Inter-Tribal Cultural Heritage Site

FIGURE 9.1 This Desert View landscape includes *Desert View Watchtower* designed by Mary Colter, 1932.
Source: Grand Canyon NPS/Michael Quinn. Flickr, (CC by 2.0).

Desert View (Figure 9.1), located within the Grand Canyon National Park (GCNP), became the National Park Service's (NPS's) first inter-tribal cultural heritage site. Its working transformation resulted from the GCNP's leadership acknowledging Native Americans' campaigns to return to ancestral homelands. GCNP developed an Inter-tribal Advisory Group (ITAG) consisting of the 11 tribes traditionally associated with the Grand Canyon—the Havasupai, Hopi, Hualapai, Navajo, Zuni, Yavapai-Apache, and five bands of Southern Paiute to implement its plans for developing inter-tribal tourism, generating conservation jobs, and teaching visitors about First Nation's cultures, land stewardship, art, and spiritual beliefs.

Desert View is situated in the Colorado Plateau province that straddles the Four Corners region, where the state boundaries of present-day Colorado, New Mexico, Arizona, and Utah meet. In 1932, Hopi artist Fred Kabotie (Naqavo'ma/Day After Day, 1900–86) was commissioned to paint murals at *Desert View Watchtower* (Figure 9.2) designed by architect and interior decorator Mary Colter (1869–1958). Colter designed *Desert View Watchtower* based on her studies and on-site observations (Figure 9.3) of architectural works created by the ancestral Puebloans, among the first people to inhabit the Four Corners region (circa 12th-century BCE). The ancestral Puebloans began constructing villages (**pueblos**) during the Basketmaker II era (1500 BCE–500 CE). Given careful observations and knowledge of the land, they achieved architectural and engineering feats during the Pueblo II and III eras (900 CE–1350 CE) in locations including *Hovenweep* (Figure 9.4) and *Cliff Palace* at

DOI: 10.4324/9781003183693-12

FIGURE 9.2 Fred Kabotie painting the *Snake Legend* at *Desert View Watchtower*. c.1932.

Source: *Fred Harvey Co. Grand Canyon NPS. Flickr, (CC by 2.0).*

FIGURE 9.3 Mary Colter conducted on-site research at *Hovenweep Castle*.

Source: *Fred Harvey Co. Grand Canyon NPS. Flickr, (CC by 2.0).*

FIGURE 9.4 Ancestral Puebloan. *Hovenweep Castle*. 1200–1300 CE.

Source: *Mobilus In Mobili. Flickr, (CC BY-SA 2.0).*

FIGURE 9.5 Ancestral Puebloan. *Cliff Palace* at Mesa Verde National Park. 1190–1260 CE.

Source: *NPS/Sandy Groves. Public Domain.*

Mesa Verde (Figure 9.5). Around the end of the 13th century, ancestral Puebloans continued their migrations to new homelands. Accrued events beginning in the 16th century resulted in the theft of indigenous homelands, including Spanish colonizers, European settlers' western expansion, discriminatory federal laws and policies, and the 1919 establishment of GCNP.

Transforming GCNP into a tourist destination, The Fred Harvey Company appointed Mary Colter to design GCNP's *Desert View Watchtower* in 1932 as a "Rest and View House" (Colter, 2015, p. 15). Colter modeled *Desert View Watchtower's* circular form from ancestral Puebloan's *Round Tower* at Mesa Verde's *Cliff Palace* and *Hovenweep's* weathered rocks. The various rocks forming *Desert View Watchtower* stemmed from Colter's mimicry of ancestral Puebloan practices of building with varied rock textures and colors. She hired Hopi artists and artisans due to their deep spiritual and historical connections to Desert View. The Hopi are descendants of ancient Puebloans. Their culture explains that the human race emerged into this world from **Siipapu**, a sacred site near the confluence of the Colorado River and Little Colorado River in the Grand Canyon. Colter (2015) envisioned Desert View as a space to educate visitors about the ancient peoples of the Colorado Plateau. Fred Kabotie designed its *Hopi Room* murals (Figure 9.6) to welcome visitors and express his people's relationship to the Grand Canyon.

GCNP's vision to transform Desert View into an inter-tribal cultural heritage site is an expansion of Colter's initial intent. NPS's (2016) leadership apologized for its past decisions that forcefully removed Native Americans from their homelands and caused pain. With the desire to make ongoing changes, ITAG expressed: "The Watchtower serves as a connection to embrace the heartbeats of our peoples and visitors far and wide

FIGURE 9.6 Four white lines painted by Fred Kabotie welcome visitors to *Desert View Watchtower*.
Source: Grand Canyon NPS/Michael Quinn. Flickr. (CC by 2.0).

with the heartbeat of the canyon …We are still here" (NPS, 2018, p. 3).

Teaching and Learning in the STEAM Artist's Studio 9.1 addresses Desert View's transformation into an inter-tribal cultural

---

Teaching and Learning in the STEAM Artist's Studio 9.1

Introduce students to *Desert View Watchtower's* working transformation into an inter-tribal cultural site. Make connections to ancestral Puebloan architecture, Fred Kabotie, Mary Colter, Hopi art and design, and advocacy using First Voices.

Essential/Guiding Questions

1. Why is *Desert View Watchtower* being transformed into an inter-tribal cultural heritage site?
2. How did Fred Kabotie's knowledge as a Hopi artist inform his Hopi Room murals? How did Mary Colter's on-site observations of ancestral Puebloan architecture inform *Desert View Watchtower's* design?

Daily Learning Targets

As a designer, I can use observations to construct an architectural model that teaches about positive transformation.

- I can incorporate materials that are prevalent in my community.
- I can make revisions to produce a balanced and unified design.
- I can describe how my observations correlate with the design I created.

National Core Arts Anchor Standards NVAS 2, 5, 8, and 11.
www.nationalartsstandards.org

Teaching for Students' Development

PK-12: (A) Discuss how the ancestral Puebloans are among the first inhabitants of the Colorado Plateau. It remains home to indigenous peoples. (B) Ask students to explain the importance of home and telling stories in their own words. Make connections to the 11 tribes traditionally associated with the Grand Canyon.

Early childhood: Young children are developing hand-eye coordination and can recognize how the placements of objects change designs. Encourage students to identify how they use (visual) sensory input as they practice stacking blocks and manipulating objects to form architectural structures, such as towers.

Middle childhood: Students are able to notice details. Have students study the characteristics of ancestral Puebloan architecture, Colter's *Desert View Watchtower*, and petroglyphs in the ancient styles of art. (See the companion website.)

Early adolescence: Middle school students can create drawings that show scale and proportion. Teach students how architects use blueprints drawn to scale to construct buildings. Ask students to sketch their architectural structures to scale to prepare their three-dimensional designs.

Adolescence: High school students can apply spatial reasoning skills to solve architectural-design problems. Show examples of ancestral Puebloan architectural structures built on boulders and cliff edges. Have students brainstorm and research ideas for building on uneven surfaces and ledges.

heritage site. Its *STEAM Amplifiers* teach about Fred Kabotie's Hopi Room; *Desert View Watchtower's* conservation; cultural appropriation; and First Voices.

STEAM AMPLIFIERS CHOICE #1—FRED KABOTIE: *HOPI ROOM'S* TEACHINGS

Fred Kabotie is an internationally acclaimed artist who dedicated his life to following the teachings of his culture. He attended a U.S. Government-mandated reservation school designed to assimilate Native American children into Euro-American culture and eradicate their languages, religious practices, and ways of life (Hortan, 2017). After experiencing physical abuse at school, Kabotie refused to attend school until age 15, when he was sent to the Santa Fe Indian School. While Kabotie attended boarding school, Mr. De Huff became its superintendent. He and his wife Elizabeth ignored government assimilation policies. They encouraged Kabotie to create art and preserve his traditional lifeway. Kabotie (1977), who was a lifelong learner, reflected "I've found that the more outside education I receive, the more I appreciate the true Hopi way" (p. 12). De Huff's advocacy for indigenous cultures ultimately resulted in

FIGURE 9.7 Fred Kabotie, *Hopi Room's Snake Legend,* 1932. The left side presents the mural before conservation and the right side shows the mural after its conservation.

Source: Grand Canyon NPS/Michael Quinn. Flickr. (CC by 2.0).

Mr. De Huff's subsequent demotion and eventual resignation. Kabotie and the De Huffs retained their close relationship.

Kabotie created *Hopi Room's Snake Legend* mural (Figures 9.2, 9.3, and 9.7) to teach Desert View's visitors about the origins of Hopi physical and spiritual life (Colter, 2015). Kabotie (1977) explained: "I painted the Snake Legend, showing that the first man to float through the canyon was a Hopi—hundreds of years before Major John Wesley Powell's historic Grand Canyon trip in 1869" (p. 49). Navigating it clockwise, the top left (north/yellow) tells the story of the Hopi father giving his son, a young man, prayer offerings in preparation for the son's journey to learn where the Colorado River's waters flow. The top right quadrant (west/turquoise) shows the young man traveling down the Colorado River in a covered wooden boat. The bottom right quadrant (south/red) presents the young man interacting with an ancient tribal people from Mesoamerica that teach him how to call the rains through their relationship with the rattlesnake. The lower left quadrant (white/east)

depicts the young man returning home with his new bride, who will become the mother of the Snake Clan.

Referencing Figure 9.2, have students observe Kabotie's *Hopi Room's Snake Legend* mural closely. Ask students to describe how Kabotie's designs teach about the origins of the Snake Clan.

STEAM AMPLIFIERS CHOICE #2—MULTIDISCIPLINARY CONSERVATION

In 2015, GCNP commissioned a multidisciplinary conservation team of engineers, archeologists, and artists to conserve *Desert View Watchtower.* Based on his examinations, engineer Doug Porter (NPS, 2017) believed that the watchtower probably began leaking soon after its construction, which caused large vertical cracks and water infiltration that produced streaking salt stains that damaged its murals (Figure 9.7). When Colter designed *Desert View Watchtower,* she used unreinforced masonry supported by a steel frame that triggered its structural problems. Today's architects accommodate the expansion and contraction of building materials. Porter explained that *Desert View Watchtower's* damage was "the result of diurnal and seasonal changes in temperature and the stresses imposed by the wind" (NPS, 2017). His conservation team selected a flexible sealant for repairs because it moves with the building, thereby reducing stress and damage.

To maintain the integrity of Fred Kabotie's murals, the conservation team minimized their work whenever possible and focused on removing accumulated dirt and salt. Kabotie's grandson,

Ed Kabotie (Okhuwa P'ing/Cloud Mountain), was part of the team. He blended conservation grade paints to conceal stains around the murals so that they remained authentic and uncompromised.

Given this information, discuss the importance of *Desert View Watchtower's* conservation. Ask students to explain why a multidisciplinary team was commissioned for the conservation work.

STEAM AMPLIFIERS CHOICE #3—CULTURAL APPROPRIATION

The aesthetic term **appropriation** describes artists' use of other artists' works. Artists appropriate for multiple reasons including to learn new skills, honor artists/designers they admire, produce new works that visibly reference inspirational ones, and gain notoriety for using already famous works. **Cultural appropriation** differs from artistic appropriation because people borrow and apply ideas outside of their own culture—generally created by a majority or dominant group. They culturally appropriate symbols they do not understand, have permission to use, and/or have interpreted inaccurately. Colter's cultural appropriation of *Desert View Watchtower* was made possible by colonialism. She (2015) conceived *Desert View Watchtower* as a site-specific re-creation of ancestral Puebloan architecture, rather than a copy, replica, or reproduction. Colter felt her design aligned with ancient Puebloans' practices because each work was original and built "according to the character of the site, the materials that could be procured and the purpose for which the building was

FIGURE 9.8 *Desert View Watchtower's Kiva Room.*
Source: Grand Canyon NPS/Michael Quinn. Flickr, *(CC by 2.0).*

intended" (Colter, 2015, p. 17). She also integrated ancestral Puebloan and Hopi architecture, art, and artifacts into *Desert View Watchtower's* design for greater authenticity (Figure 9.8).

Have students compare and contrast appropriation and cultural appropriation. Explain how non-native American artists have culturally appropriated Native American designs and produced works that are stereotypical, inaccurate, insulting, and/or used without permission. Teach the many benefits of authentic Native American art and design.

STEAM AMPLIFIERS CHOICE #4—FIRST VOICES

Our STEAM curriculum will incorporate First Voices, histories, and cultural perspectives. Teaching with First Voices is essential to avoid misinterpretations resulting from not possessing First Nation languages, spiritual knowledge, cultural paradigms, and histories. The ancient peoples of the Colorado Plateau developed advanced farming, engineering, and architectural skills. Students can study how the ancestral Puebloans and their descendants have lived and interacted in the Colorado Plateau for centuries and how Colonialism resulted in a forced boarding school system for Native Americans and produced industrial mining that has poisoned Native American lands (Ed Kabotie, personal communication, August 2022). These continue to impact the lives of Native Americans today. Students can brainstorm actions to make positive changes to reverse the impacts of colonialism like GCNP has done by transforming Desert View into an inter-tribal cultural heritage site. Our curriculum will teach students that indigenous peoples are not people of the past, as ITAG's statement emphasized "We are still here" (NPS, 2018, p. 3).

This book's companion website provides links to access First Voice resources and artworks including Grand Canyon Conservancy videos for students to observe artistic practices by First Nation artists including Hopi jeweler Lyle Balenquah, Navajo textile weaver Florence Riggs, and Hopi-Diné basket weaver Iva Honyestewa and the Kabotie family's creative works, including Ed Kabotie's edutainment social media sites that showcase his music, his band Tha 'Yoties' performances, and artworks (Figure 9.9) addressing topics of spirituality, cultural achievements, and social injustices including arsenic contaminations and water depletion on indigenous lands.

FIGURE 9.9 Ed Kabotie's, *Confluence*, 2021, describes: "The Confluence of the Little Colorado River and the Great Colorado illustrate the powerful merging of female and male energies. Through their union, life is enhanced and multiplied as their waters carry sustenance down river…" (personal communication, August 2022).
Source: © Ed Kabotie

MOVING FULL STEAM AHEAD...

This chapter described Desert View's relationship to the ancient people of the Grand Canyon region and its working transformation into an inter-tribal cultural heritage site resulting from First Nations' advocacy. We learned how Mary Colter designed *Desert View Watchtower* using observations of innovative ancestral Puebloan architecture and included Fred Kabotie's murals to teach its visitors about Hopi physical and spiritual life. Desert View's working transformation into an inter-tribal cultural heritage site brings awareness to the need for additional sites to permeate North America as resources to see and hear First Nations' perspectives. This chapter completes Part III of this book with its focus on the artistic behavior of observation. The next chapter discusses Camille Utterback and her interactive designs. It begins Part IV of this book with its teaching on the artistic behavior of imagination and wonderment.

References

Colter, M. E. J. (2015). *Watchtower at Desert View.* Grand Canyon Conservancy.

Hortan, J. L. (2017). *Art for an undivided earth: The American Indian movement generation.* Duke University Press.

Kabotie, F. (1977). *Fred Kabotie, Hopi Indian artist: An autobiography told with Bill Belknap.* Museum of Northern Arizona/Northland Press.

National Park Service. (2016). *Re-dedication of Desert View Watchtower.* [Video]. https://www.nps.gov/grca/planyourvisit/desert-view-watchtower-rededication-may-22-2016.htm

National Park Service. (2017). *Partners in preservation—Angelyn Bass and Douglas Porter—Episode 5.* [Video]. https://www.nps.gov/media/video/view.htm?id=BE67A135-C41C-47CD-A6FD-97FD4E15F7D7&utm_source=Audio&utm_medium=website&utm_campaign=experience_more

National Park Service. (2018). *Grand Canyon National Park—Desert View inter-tribal cultural heritage site plan/environmental assessment.* https://parkplanning.nps.gov/document.cfm?parkID=65&projectID=53814&documentID=89530

PART IV

Artists' Lessons to Thrive! Imagination and Wonderment

Chapter 10

Camille Utterback

Interactive Designs that Move Us

FIGURE 10.1 Romy Achituv and Camille Utterback. *Text Rain*, 1999.

Source: Image courtesy of Camille Utterback from the Boston Cyberarts Festival in 2001. Text Rain is in the collection of the Smithsonian American Art Museum. © Romy Achituv and Camille Utterback.

Camille Utterback is an interactive artist who applies her knowledge of coding and electronics to write software and create digital installations. Utterback's technical abilities combined with her artistic skills and imaginative ideas empower her to bring her innovative artistic visions to life. Acknowledging that technology can sometimes feel isolating, Utterback writes software programs that encourage human-computer interactions. She prefers to create her own technical products and avoids predeveloped ones designed for other applications because they confine what her art can become. Utterback explained:

> By refiguring the possibilities for interaction with digital media, I question and explore the space between the symbolic and the corporeal; between the virtual and the real. By creating poetic relationships between these spaces I hope to engage people both emotionally and viscerally.
>
> (Utterback, 2022, para. 7)

Utterback's technological installations transform people from passive spectators to active participants.

DOI: 10.4324/9781003183693-14

When developing new artworks, Utterback anticipates people's behaviors and writes software rules that predetermine viewers' possible physical responses to her interactive artworks. They are void of signs that say touch here or move in this direction. Rather, participants experience wonderment as they intuitively figure out her artworks' functions by moving their bodies in explorative ways and predicting what the artworks might do next.

Utterback's interactive artworks have been inspired by her master's thesis, *Text Rain* (1999) that she created with Romy Achituv (Figure 10.1). They developed *Text Rain* at a time when computer technologies were much slower and most people had not experienced computer projection screens. Using live, black-and-white video feed projected onto a screen, *Text Rain* participants see mirrored images of themselves. Colorful letters, words, and phrases from Evan Zimroth's poem *Talk, You* flow within the space. *Text Rain* encourages people to catch, lift, and drop letters. The letters do not fall randomly. The artists designed *Text Rain's* software rules so that the poem's letters float downward and then bounce upward when they come in contact with darkened masses on the screen. Participants realize that the longer they stay in place, the more words and phrases from the poem appear, causing them to use their bodies as instruments to collect information and their minds to interpret the text. The more people interact with *Text Rain*, the more dynamic the work becomes.

Text Rain resulted from Achituv and Utterback's interests in activating people's bodies through technological works when people were limited to using their fingertips to interact with technology through a mouse and keyboard. They are credited as the inventors of *Text Rain's* video tracking software programming that received a 2004 US patent. The patent legally recognizes their invention of a simple real-time method for facilitating wireless interactions between humans and textual data. *Text Rain* puts spectators at ease performing visceral movements next to complete strangers—removing normal boundaries that occur in public places. Play becomes natural in a museum environment as participants catch letters in their mouths and on their outstretched arms. Words assembled on large surfaces reveal the poem's phrases and sentences. The longer spectators stay still, the more words form. In 2015, the Smithsonian American Art Collection acquired *Text Rain* because of the artists' ability to develop aesthetically pleasing cutting-edge technology, change people's behaviors within museum settings, and produce an interactive artwork that remains highly relevant decades after its invention (Nodjimbadem, 2015).

Given our learning on Camille Utterback and, *Text Rain*, we will apply *Teaching and Learning in the STEAM Artist's Studio 10.1's* information to invite students to create interactive video sensing artworks using MIT Scratch's (n.d.) free activity guides and instructional videos (Figure 10.2). **Video sensing** offers students exciting ways to develop interactive-screen technology artworks triggered by their physical motions. The *STEAM Amplifiers* teach about algorithms, coding, the Seeing AI app, and interactive art installation etiquette.

Teaching and Learning in the STEAM Artist's Studio 10.1

Introduce students to Camille Utterback and *Text Rain* that she created with Romy Achituv. Ask students to explain poetry's role in *Text Rain's* design. Then, visit the Scratch website to view its video sensing extension activity guide. Scratch's video sensing extension accesses a computing device's camera application to capture live videos. Students will use the extension's blocks of code to program behaviors such as the levels of sensitivity that the camera will respond to their actions and create a **sprite**—a computer graphic image that fits within a rectangle—to animate their videos. Students can choose from Scratch's collection of preexisting sprite characters and objects and/or draw original ones. Scratch's (n.d.) website offers an activity guide tutorial for students to learn how to animate a sprite. Additionally, students can use Scratch's text-to-speech coding block, choose from its sound collection, and make original recordings. Given their selections, they will program their sprites' behaviors and use their bodies as instruments—like Achituv and Utterback planned for *Text Rain*—as part of their video sensing performance. (Note: An unplugged alternative to this lesson is for students to perform with a light source (projector and/or flashlight) behind a white sheet (like a shadow puppet performance) with cutout letters, words, and handmade sprites and use their bodies to perform with them.

Essential/Guiding Questions

1. Why does Utterback develop artworks that make technology less isolating? How do her creations spark people's imagination and wonderment?
2. What role does interactivity play in *Text Rain's* function as an artwork? How does it shape the artwork's meaning and influence people's behaviors?

Daily Learning Targets

As artists, we can develop an interactive performance inspired by a STEAM-themed poem of our choice using Scratch's video sensing extension.

- We can organize blocks of code to prepare for our performance.
- We can incorporate sprites (image and text symbols) to animate our poem inspiration.
- We can integrate audio components such as spoken words, music, and sound effects to enhance our work.
- We can use our bodies as instruments to interact with the sprite animations and sounds we have programmed for our performance.

We can participate in a class critique to discuss our interactive performance and its effectiveness in communicating its message.

National Core Arts Anchor Standards NVAS 2, 6, 9, and 10.
www.nationalartsstandards.org

Teaching for Students' Development

PK-12: (A) Present Scratch's tutorials on how to use its video sensing extension. Inform students that they can follow along to learn its steps and then make changes to reflect their design interests. (B) Have students brainstorm ways to integrate effective gestures to interact with the sprites they select for their poetry-inspired performance.

Early childhood: Young children are pre-readers and beginning readers. Writing prompts assist them in story development. Write prompts such as "on a sunny day" to facilitate students' development of a collaborative poem for their interactive performance. Students will add new lines of text that build on the previous ones. When ready to create their video sensing, read coding aloud and model directions for students to follow.

Middle childhood: Students are interested in hobbies and can integrate personal interests to develop poems and interactive performances that spark wonderment. Check for students' understanding and assist them in following steps as needed.

Early adolescence: Middle school students value friendships and are becoming more aware of global issues. Ask students to consider ways to develop their poems using age-appropriate global influences and design-interactive performances with their classmates.

Adolescence: High school students understand how products can be created in response to a philosophical belief. Explain how Achituv and Utterback created *Text Rain* as an innovative artwork for people to use their bodies as instruments and interact with technology. Encourage students to integrate a philosophical belief of their choice into their interactive performance.

STEAM AMPLIFIERS CHOICE #1—ALGORITHMS

An **algorithm** is a set of instructions needed to complete a task or solve a problem. Computer scientists develop "plugged" algorithms that are executed by computer devices, websites, and apps. **Coding**, formed from algorithms, is written in a programming language that the computer understands and can apply in the appropriate sequences to produce accurate results. The coding Achituv and Utterback invented for *Text Rain* was awarded a US patent because of its originality.

We will teach students that not all algorithms require technology. In everyday

FIGURE 10.2 Eric Schilling @Speak Visually demonstrates video sensing using live video footage and a coded sprite that meows, glides, and changes colors in response to people's actions.

Source: Courtesy of MIT Scratch. Scratch Team. YouTube, Video Sensing! Create-Along LIVE: Let's make Scratch projects together!

life, we utilize "unplugged" algorithms to complete tasks such as tying shoelaces. Algorithms are most efficient when students develop them using organized, clear, and logical steps to produce intended results. Students will practice creating precise instructions in clear language with finite steps for their peers to follow. For example, students can plan unplugged algorithm tasks to guide their gesture actions to interact with imaginary sprites (symbols) for this chapter's *Teaching and Learning in the STEAM Artist's Studio* and then advance to using plugged algorithms.

STEAM AMPLIFIERS CHOICE #2—GETTING STARTED WITH CODING

Coding is a precise programming language that requires practice (Figure 10.3). K-12 schools and colleges are teaching beginning students how to code using blocks of code, such as Blocky Code Blocks. Students can choose from an existing selection of blocks that have built-in coding written in languages such as JavaScript and Python. They arrange the interlocking blocks as tools in a workspace to perform a sequence

FIGURE 10.3 Eighth-grade students combine their studies of algorithms, icon design, math skills, and coding.

Source: Courtesy of Educators' Cooperative Teachers Brandi Hodge and Mike Mitchell.

of coded actions. Their "hidden" codes consist of written words and symbols. A block of code can generate repeated actions. Some codes are **conditional** on allowing for changes. **"If"** and **"If, else"** **statements** are developed to provide users with options. "If" is the most basic **conditional statement**. If a condition is true, the computer will run a block of code for an action to occur, such as "if at an easel, pick up a paintbrush." "If, else" statements provide further options. When false, the program will execute the else action. For example, if a user arrives at a drawing horse instead of an easel, the else statement would read "pick up a piece of charcoal" instead of a paintbrush. Programmers can develop longer sequences of else statements to provide

greater choices. The programmer defines the appropriate statements and actions to match the circumstances. Students can work with blocks of code on websites including Scratch, Code.org, and Blocky Games as foundations to learn a coding language. The Internet also contains many game-based, unplugged-coding activities that teach coding skills.

STEAM AMPLIFIERS CHOICE #3—SEEING AI: AN ASSISTIVE TECHNOLOGY

Text is an important component in *Text Rain*. Assistive technologies assist people with disabilities and reading barriers in understanding and accessing text (Francesc et al., 2019). Microsoft's Seeing AI is a free intelligent camera app available on iOS for iPhone or iPad that uses an Optical Character Recognition (OCR) tool to convert text to speech. Its narration abilities make previously inaccessible information accessible. Seeing AI uses artificial intelligence to think and problem-solve like humans. Designed by Saqib Shaikh, a software engineer, who lost his vision at age seven, Seeing AI transforms short text, documents, and handwriting into audio speech descriptions (Desmond, 2020). It can read students' handwritten poems, class signs, journal writings on STEAM, photographs, and live video captures. For example, Seeing AI interpreted Figure 10.1 as "Probably a person holding the hand up." Given demonstrations and practice using Seeing AI, students will discuss the benefits of developing artificial intelligence to generate accessible text and read visual data.

STEAM AMPLIFIERS CHOICE #4—INTERACTIVE ART INSTALLATION ETIQUETTE

Museums are making their spaces more interactive so that visitors can engage with artworks, participate in social experiences, and form personal connections to artworks and museums. Students will research museum etiquette practices including (a) no touching the art and walls; (b) no eating, drinking, and phone calls; (c) checking bags; (d) speaking with quiet, indoor voices; and (e) taking photographs only when permitted and never using a flash. Students will analyze museum collections' different built environment spaces for displaying art to compare and contrast their functions. They will analyze the qualities that foster successful interactive spaces compared to ones in which visitors must keep their distance. For example, the Smithsonian and other museums display *Text Rain* in open environments removed from fragile objects so that visitors can experience wonderment as they move their bodies before its screen and interact with others (Figure 10.4). Given their final analysis, students will determine how museum etiquette helps preserve artworks and how well-designed interactive spaces enhance museum experiences.

FIGURE 10.4 Interactive art installations, like Romy Achituv and Camille Utterback's *Text Rain*, encourage museum visitors to move their bodies. *Source: Collection of Smithsonian American Art Museum. © Romy Achituv and Camille Utterback.*

MOVING FULL STEAM AHEAD...

This chapter described how interactive artists Romy Achituv and Camille Utterback created *Text Rain* and were recognized as the inventors for its video tracking software that received a US patent. Their groundbreaking work has reshaped human's interactions in museums. Since *Text Rain's* production, Utterback has continued to develop innovative digital installations that spark people's imaginations and encourage human interactions. Inspired by *Text Rain*, we learned about algorithms, coding, the Seeing AI app, and interactive art installation etiquette. In the next chapter, we will study George Lucas and the role of imagination and wonderment in his development of the three *Star Wars* trilogies.

References

Desmond, N. (2020, August 20). Microsoft's Seeing AI founder Saqib Shaikh is speaking at Sight Tech Global. *TechCrunch.* https://techcrunch.com/2020/08/20/microsofts-seeing-ai-founder-saqib-shaikh-is-speaking-at-sight-tech-global/

Francesc, P., Subosa, M., Rivas, A., & Valverde, P. (2019). Artificial intelligence in education:

Challenges and opportunities for sustainable development. *UNESCO.* https://unesdoc.unesco.org/ark:/48223/pf0000366994?posInSet=9&queryId=4a437600-5100-4206-a5e7-0c552668d1d1

Nodjimbadem, K. (2015, September 23). This interactive installation rains a poem down on viewers. *Smithsonian Magazine.* https://www.smithsonianmag.com/innovation/this-interactive-installation-rains-poem-down-viewers-180956713/?no-ist

Scratch. (n.d.). *Activity guides.* https://scratch.mit.edu/ideas

Utterback, C. (2022). *Statement.* Camille Utterback. http://camilleutterback.com/vitae/statement/

Chapter 11

George Lucas

A Lasting Force

FIGURE 11.1 George Lucas's *Empire Strikes Back* (1983) characters Luke Skywalker and Darth Vader fight with lightsabers.
Source: Star Wars YouTube Channel. "Star Wars: The Digital Movie Collection." Fair Use.

"A long time ago in a galaxy far, far away...." begins the infamous opening crawl that introduces movie audiences to George Lucas's *Star Wars* space adventure. Referred to as the greatest story of all time (Kaminski, 2008), Lucas's three-trilogy saga centers on a mythological universal power he named the force. In the original trilogy, Lucas's protagonist Luke Skywalker (Figure 11.1) learns the force is "an energy field created by all living things," from his mentor Obi-Wan Kenobi who guides him to Grand Master Yoda (Figure 11.2) to undertake Jedi training. Jedi Masters and their allies fight to preserve goodness from evil forces led by the antagonist Darth Vader (Figure 11.1).

Lucas spent three years writing the screenplay for the 1977 film, producing multiple storyline drafts. Developing its characters and plot was a process of discovery. Initially, Lucas did not know all of the answers (Kaminski, 2008; Life Magazine, 2019). His efforts made the *Star Wars* characters believable and rife with human emotions. *Star Wars* became an enormous success breaking previous box office records. Audiences wanted more. Over a 42-year span, Lucas developed Episodes IV–VI, (1977–83), the prequel trilogy's Episodes I–III, (1999–2005), and the sequel trilogy's Episodes VII–IX (2015–19).

Lucas drew inspirations from the pop culture of his youth including the *Flash Gordon* serial, westerns, comic books, and science fiction works, as well as the artistic films he studied in college including Japanese director Akira Kurosawa's Samurai films (Kaminski, 2012; Seitz, 2002). As creative director for his *Star Wars* saga, he made artistic choices about

DOI: 10.4324/9781003183693-15

FIGURE 11.2 In the *Empire Strikes Back* (1983), Yoda uses the *force* to raise Luke Skywalker's XWing Starfighter.

Source: Star Wars YouTube Channel. "The Empire Strikes Back—Star Wars: The Digital Movie Collection." Fair Use.

all aspects of his films. Consistent with the revisions Lucas made to his original screenplay, his production team developed preliminary sketches, animatics, and multiple models of spacecraft, creatures, and scenes to produce stunning results.

Special effects supervisor John Stears won an Academy Award for Best Visual Effects for *Episode IV: A New Hope*. His special effects included *Star Wars'* lightsabers (energy swords, Figure 11.1) and the Death Star space station that destroyed entire planets. Stears also designed the beloved robots R2-D2 and C-3PO (Figure 11.3). Makeup artist Stuart Freeborn designed *Star Wars'* iconic characters Yoda, Chewbacca, and Jabba the Hut. He created the 26″ Yoda puppet with real human hair and latex to mimic skin. Puppeteer and actor Frank Oz, renowned from *Sesame Street* and *The Muppets* (see Chapter 15), performed the Yoda puppet and developed Yoda's distinct character voice. Through advances in computer-generated imagery (CGI) and animation, animator Rob Coleman gave Yoda's character dynamic physical actions that were impossible in the original trilogy. Academy Award-winning composer John Williams augmented *Star Wars'* emotional appeal with his soundtracks. Williams's **leitmotifs**—repeated musical sound clips

FIGURE 11.3 Droids C-3PO and R2-D2 play prominent roles in Lucas's trilogies.

Source: Division of Cultural and Community Life, National Museum of American History, Smithsonian Institution.

integrated throughout the films—provided emotional cues that connected audiences to characters and events, such as the uplifting *Yoda's Theme* and dramatic *The Imperial March (Darth Vader's Theme)*.

Given the *Star Wars* saga's success as a multimedia franchise, it seems difficult to imagine that Lucas struggled to find a movie studio to produce his visionary *Episode 4: A New Hope*. Through the support of an executive at 20th-Century Fox, Lucas turned his preliminary ideas into the space fantasy film he desired (Life Magazine, 2019). His pivotal work changed the film industry so much that the Library of Congress's (2022) National Film Registry recognized and preserved Episodes IV and V as films that are "culturally, historically, or aesthetically significant."

For *Teaching and Learning in the STEAM Artist's Studio 11.1*, we will apply what

Teaching and Learning in the STEAM Artist's Studio 11.1

Introduce students to George Lucas's imaginative storytelling methods and show *Star Wars* movie clips. Describe how Lucas wrote multiple drafts of his *Star Wars* screenplay. Lucas's production team developed sketches and models to bring *Star Wars'* film characters, spacecraft, and environments to life. Apply this information to teach students how to develop a script and storyboard.

Essential/Guiding Questions

1. Why do artists like Lucas make revisions to their work? How can the process of making revisions enhance artists' imaginative ideas?
2. Lucas worked with a team of experts to bring his films to life. How did their collaborative efforts benefit the *Star Wars* trilogies?

Daily Learning Targets

As an artist, I can use my imagination to create an original script and illustrate it in a storyboard format.

- I can plan a logical sequence of events.
- I can incorporate the necessary scenes and characters to spark wonderment.
- I can unify my script's content with my storyboard's illustrations.

I can make revisions to my works to convey my artistic ideas and imaginative visions.

National Core Arts Anchor Standards NVAS 2, 5, 8, and 10. www.nationalartsstandards.org

Teaching for Students' Development

PK-12: (A) Demonstrate how to write a script and create a storyboard to illustrate scenes. (B) Teach safety procedures as applicable.

   Early childhood: Young learners are developing language and manipulative skills. Break learning tasks into small, manageable ones to help students acquire literacy skills and visual/media arts techniques.

   Middle childhood: Students can work more independently. Continue using smaller steps to guide students in creating scripts and media artworks to foster students' independence.

   Early adolescence: Middle school students have a deep interest in visual culture and can apply personal connections to their scripts and storyboards. Invite students to brainstorm how to integrate visual culture inspirations to create stories that are imaginative, entertaining, and/or informative about issues of the day.

Adolescence: Students can study professions associated with media arts including robotics and green-screen technologies. Have students identify how special effects bring imaginative content to life and spark audience's wonderment.

we have learned about Lucas and how he honed his imagination to create epic trilogies that have sparked people's imaginations and sense of wonderment since the 1970s. The *STEAM Amplifiers* teach about kinetic art bots, robots, green-screen compositing, and the *WISER Consumer Model Questions for Visual Culture Studies*.

their experimentations, students will identify how varying placements and selections of objects produce changes in the bots' designs and the scribbles they produce. Have students transform their bots' scribbles into a complete artwork that adds meaning to their bot's design—such as a galaxy background, a planet's surface, or an atmosphere.

STEAM AMPLIFIERS CHOICE #1—KINETIC ART BOTS

R2-D2 and C-3PO serve as inspirations for students to learn about bots. A **bot** has random kinetic motions driven by a motor and an electric circuit (Figure 11.4). Its off-balanced form causes it to move when students insert a battery into an attached motor connected to the circuit wires of a battery holder case. (See directions on the companion website.) Students can compare their bots' playful movements with R2-D2 and C-3PO's use of humor in the *Star Wars* trilogies.

Bots can be developed into characters. Encourage students to produce multiple art bot prototypes and try using alternative materials and drawing instruments. Given

STEAM AMPLIFIERS CHOICE #2—ROBOTS

Even though many people visualize robots as humanoid characters like C-3PO, they come in many shapes and sizes. A **robot** is a physical machine with artificial intelligence that people program with a **controller** (computer/chip) to perform complex operations (Figure 11.5). Bots differ from robots because they do not possess artificial intelligence and cannot be programmed. The **robotic paradigm** "sense, think, and act"

FIGURE 11.4 Students make collaborative scribbles with their art bots. (cropped photograph)
Source: Franklin Park Library. Flickr, (CC BY 2.0).

FIGURE 11.5 These in-progress student robots reveal the hardware needed to operate them.
Source: Fabrice Florin. Flickr, (CC BY-SA 2.0).

describes robots' autonomous behaviors (Siegel, 2003). **Sensing** is a robot's ability to collect data to read its surroundings using sensors such as a camera, compass, and distance-measuring lidar. **Thinking** explains a robot's intelligence in processing the information it has received to make decisions and plan its next actions within an environment. The robot's intelligence separates it from electromechanical devices. **Acting** occurs when the robot performs its intended operations, such as using its motors to generate the movements it was programmed to do and/or make adaptations resulting from its sensing and thinking abilities.

    Roboticists work to improve robots' performances and make them more responsive to human needs by writing algorithms that enable robots to adapt to changes. Their work has inspired the integration of robots in classrooms and makerspaces so that students can learn how to program and manipulate educational robots, such as the Finch 2.0 robot (PK-16) and the Lego® Mindstorms® Robot Inventor (ages 10+). Learning robotics also introduces students to computer science coding (see Chapter 10) with simplified block forms and/or languages such as Python. When purchasing robots is cost-prohibitive, technology grants may provide funding. As alternatives to working with actual robots, students can study their types and functions (the robotic paradigm) as inspirations to create original robot drawings, animations, and sculptures.

STEAM AMPLIFIERS CHOICE #3 — GREEN-SCREEN COMPOSITING

Chroma key compositing describes green (Figure 11.6) and blue screen visual effect techniques used to change

FIGURE 11.6 High school students edit a green-screen recording.

Source: Photo by Allison Shelley/The Verbatim Agency for EDUimages. (CC BY-NC 4.0).

the main image(s) before a monochromatic screen in a photograph or video. The inserted background replaces the monochromatic one to show something different—such as bees flying in space (Figure 11.7). The original *Star Wars* trilogy is filled with special effects created with a monochromatic blue screen background that brought Lucas's otherworldly scenes to life. Lucas's team excelled at blue screen techniques without the benefits of today's technologies. They manually added masking to remove the blue screen background around the main object—such as a spacecraft exploding—and inserted a

FIGURE 11.7 This stop-motion animation frame using green-screen technologies includes an inserted NASA image and students' bee sculptures.

Source: NASA's Scientific Visualization Studio. Public Domain. Monica Leister, Joshua Harper, and Author, teachers.

new background—an image of outer space. They then composited different pieces of film together using an optical printer so that the finalized product presented the desired action scene—an epic space battle.

Green/blue screens are well-suited for chroma key compositing because their colors contrast against people's skin tones. Apps, such as *Stop Motion Studio Pro* and *Do Ink*, remove the green/blue background and replace it with a transparent one. Students then select the image or video background of their choice and the app will composite it. Quality lighting is essential. Lighting should be even to avoid shadows. Color variations on the screen, including shadows and wrinkles, reduce the background removal effectiveness. The selected green/blue screen will need to match the intended depth of field. For example, a larger screen will be necessary to produce full-body shots. If a screen is unavailable, students can film small scale-projects using green/blue paper or cloth as a background. Students can use inspirations from their studies of *Star Wars* and storytelling to develop creative chroma key compositing projects.

STEAM AMPLIFIERS CHOICE #4—WISER VISUAL CULTURE STUDIES

Star Wars' multimedia merchandise includes action-figure toys, clothing, Lego® sets, and video games. These products and their marketing campaigns align with visual culture studies that teach students how to become informed consumers of products and information.

The *WISER Consumer Model Questions for Visual Culture Studies* first introduced in the textbook *Teaching and Learning in Art Education: Cultivating Students' Potential from Pre-K Through High School* (Sickler-Voigt, 2020) presents questions that teachers can adapt to guide students in learning how to read the evidence and possible hidden messages in visual culture to form greater understandings. It contains three parts: wise investing, sales, and end results. (See additional model questions on this book's companion website.)

1. **Wise investing** prompts students to critically examine a work's content and message from the perspective of a possible consumer or user.
   - What is this *Star Wars* product about? What are its key features?
2. **Sales** has students analyze how marketers aim to sell a product or idea to consumers based on the information they collected during wise investing.
   - How do the *Star Wars* products' multimedia components (characters, costumes, set/background designs, and sounds) tell a fuller story? Given this information, to what degree does this *Star Wars* product persuade its target audience?
3. **End results** call upon students to decide if there are advantages or disadvantages in using or believing in the product or idea presented based on their thorough examinations and collections of evidence.
   - In which ways could you communicate what you have learned about this *Star Wars* product and its idea to others? Which external factors, if any, influenced your final judgment?

MOVING FULL STEAM AHEAD...

This chapter described how George Lucas applied his imagination and the pop culture influences of his youth and university studies to develop his *Star Wars* trilogies and production of multimedia *Star Wars* products. His films became global sensations that have sparked audiences' imaginations and wonderment. Their study connects to teachings on bots, robots, green-screen compositing, and WISER visual culture studies. In the next chapter, we will learn about Jenova Chen and Kellee Santiago and their creation of the video game *Flower* that they designed as art.

References

Kaminski, M. (2008). *The secret history of Star Wars: The art of storytelling and the making of a modern epic*. Legacy Books.

Kaminski, M. (2012). Under the influence of Akira Kurosawa: The visual style of George Lucas. In D. Brode, & L. Deyneka (Eds.), *Myth media and culture in Star Wars: An anthology* (pp. 83–99). The Scarecrow Press.

Library of Congress. (2022). *Selections from the National Film Registry: About this collection.* https://www.loc.gov/collections/selections-from-the-national-film-registry/about-this-collection/

Life Magazine. (Editor). (2019). George Lucas and the making of Star Wars: How the Skywalker saga began. *Life Magazine, 97.*

Seitz, M. Z. (2002). *Star Wars: The A list: The National Society of Film Critics' 100 Essential Films. Library of Congress.* https://www.loc.gov/static/programs/national-film-preservation-board/documents/star_wars.pdf

Sickler-Voigt, D. C. (2020). *Teaching and learning in art education: Cultivating students' potential from pre-K through high school.* Routledge.

Siegel, M. (2003). The sense-think-act paradigm revisited. 1st International Workshop on Robotic Sensing. *ROSE' 03.* doi: 10.1109/ROSE.2003.1218700.

Chapter 12

Jenova Chen and Kellee Santiago

The Art of Video Games

FIGURE 12.1 Jenova Chen, Kellee Santiago, *Flower*, 2007, video game for SONY PS3.

Source: Smithsonian American Art Museum. © 2008 Sony Computer Entertainment American LLC. Flower is a registered trademark of Sony Computer Entertainment America LLC. Developed by thatgamecompany.

Petals glide through the wind accompanied by a rhythmic musical score that guides them through expansive fields and urban spaces in the illuminated dreamscapes Jenova Chen and Kellee Santiago created for their highly-acclaimed video game *Flower* (Figure 12.1). Chen and Santiago design video games as artworks that generate emotional responses (Smithsonian American Art Museum, 2012). They founded thatgamecompany with the intention of creating games with universal appeal that produce previously-unimagined sensory experiences (Innovation Stuntmen, 2010). *Flower's* guiding concept began with Chen's wonderment and amazement with California's expansive green hills (Smithsonian American Art

Museum, 2012). Growing up in Shanghai, Chen had not experienced vast open spaces. He and Santiago wanted to develop a game that captured the emotional sensations of exploring rolling grass hills for the first time.

Flower took two years to develop—with 18 months spent on preproduction (Dugan, 2010). Normally, preproduction begins with play mechanics; however, Chen and Santiago's team designed *Flower's* emotions, art, and sound first. Santiago explained:

> We wanted to … start with just the emotion that we want the player to get while they're playing it. And then not have any preconceived notions about what kind of game

DOI: 10.4324/9781003183693-16

that will be, and discover it as we're making it.

(Innovation Stuntmen, 2010, para. 3)

Developing *Flower's* prototypes, they imagined different possibilities to actualize their goals. Honesty, compromise, and listening to others' input were essential to their games' development and success (Dugan, 2010).

Flower starts in a dull gray room. An isolated flower pot sits before a window with shattered glass. Players witness a bustling city filled with gray buildings, cranes, and excessive traffic before entering a flower's dream of paradise. The game progresses into a serene world where players collect flower petals guided by the wind. The petals dip into swaying grasses and fly above the planes. Sights, sounds, and feelings abound in the game's multisensory environments. *Flower* has an autobiographical component that connects to Chen's experiences. While he greatly admired nature's beauty, Chen also missed Shanghai's city life (Innovation Stuntmen, 2010).

Artists draw on their life and time, and reflect on that…. As designers, we have to think about what we want to share with our audience, what we want to tell them, otherwise we're only wasting their time.

(Kumar, 2009, para 16)

Flower expresses the need for humans to find a harmonious balance between the earth's natural elements and the built environment. The game's wind turbines demonstrate how to reduce humanity's carbon footprint.

Chen and Santiago produced the game they intended to create. *Flower* stimulates peaceful emotions as well as empathy and concern when abandoned electrical currents harm the petals. Chen and Santiago's design reduces gaming stress as players do not earn points, follow complex directions, and worry about time limits. Ultimately, *Flower* imparts its players with the gifts of art, beauty, and awe-inspiring emotions.

Teaching and Learning in the STEAM Artist's Studio 12.1 is driven by Chen and Santiago's innovative and imaginative ideas for gaming development. We can apply its information as we introduce students to game design programs. The *STEAM Amplifiers* teach about video game design, aesthetic inquiry, gaming music, and engineering wind turbines.

Teaching and Learning in
the STEAM Artist's Studio 12.1

Introduce students to *Flower* and its roles as a video game and an artwork that spark wonderment. Have students discuss the importance of imagination, quality design, and teams planning, communicating, and collaborating during game development and why Chen and Santiago invested so much time in *Flower's* preproduction. During their game's preproduction, ask student teams to apply their imaginations, communicate their ideas, listen to teammates, and make compromises. (An unplugged alternative to this lesson is to create a handmade game that is an artwork.)

Essential/Guiding Questions

1. Chen and Santiago's *Flower* stimulates imagination and wonderment. How did their artistic intentions and collaborative processes make *Flower* the game that it is?
2. Why is it important for designers like Chen and Santiago to consider a game's audience during game development?

Daily Learning Targets

As designers, we can use code to create an original video game that we perceive as art.

- We can design the type of video game of our choice (i.e., jumping game, maze) using programs such as ScratchJr, Scratch, and Code.org.
- We can design characters that align with our game's intentions.
- We can develop a game environment that gives the impression of an artistic setting.
- We can integrate character and other applicable movements.
- We can select appropriate music and sound effects.
- We can integrate scoring, if it is appropriate for our game.

National Core Arts Anchor Standards NVAS 1, 4, 9, and 10.
www.nationalartsstandards.org

Teaching for Students' Development

PK-12: (A) Have students discuss their favorite games and the qualities that make them fun, artistic, and imaginative. (B) Encourage students to play physical and digital games, draw, and brainstorm ideas to assist with their game development.

Early childhood: Young learners' reading skills impact their abilities to understand and follow written directions to code video games. Introduce age-appropriate programs such as ScratchJr. and Code.org designed for prereaders and beginning readers.

Middle childhood: Students may need assistance reading written directions and using blocks of code. Work toward students' independent attainment of these skills through practice and positive reinforcement.

Early adolescence: Middle schoolers have become more skillful in research. Provide guidance and resources to facilitate collaborative student research on gaming design.

Adolescence: Students continue to hone their research skills and can research gaming careers and techniques. Utilize class discussions and presentations for students to share their research findings.

STEAM AMPLIFIERS CHOICE #1—DESIGNING GAMES FOR THE FUTURE

Flower (Figure 12.2) is one of many games sold in the consumer market. The global gaming industry has generated approximately $160 billion in a single year and continues to grow with people of all ages playing on mobile devices, consoles, and computers (Field Level Media, 2020). With gaming's popularity, more skilled game developers are needed to meet increased market demands. Preparing for the future, students can use free programs that teach game coding including ScratchJr (Ages 5–7), Scratch (Ages 8–16+), and Code.org (Ages 4–18). *Hour of Code* (2022) activities designed for all ages encourage students to practice age-appropriate gaming and coding skills in 60-minute intervals. Students ages 13+ might also try Code.org's Game Lab. Students can use these resources in class and during their free time. Their formats incorporate drag-and-drop code blocks and/or apply languages such as JavaScript and Python to implement game actions including game controls, character designs, movements, sounds, and scoring. Students can work with the programs' existing built-in features and create original design components.

STEAM AMPLIFIERS CHOICE #2—VIDEO GAMES AS ART

Chen and Santiago designed *Flower's* aesthetic and emotional appeals using imagination, wonderment, and technical skills. *Flower* is beautiful because beauty is necessary to produce the feelings of living each flower's dream (Figure 12.3). Chen explained: "If the goal of the game is to make player(s) aware of the beauty of something in our daily life, we will certainly make it as beautiful as possible" (Samyn, 2008). Individuals need to play *Flower* to appreciate it as a complete artwork enriched with painterly landscapes and a soothing musical score.

The Smithsonian Museum of American Art was one of the first major museums that added video games—including *Flower*—to its permanent art collection. It values gaming innovations and recognizes video games as unique art forms that differ

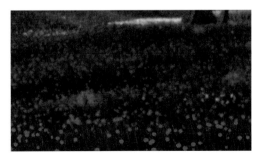

FIGURE 12.2 Jenova Chen, Kellee Santiago, *Flower*, 2007, video game for SONY PS3.
Source: Smithsonian American Art Museum. © 2008 Sony Computer Entertainment American LLC. Flower is a registered trademark of Sony Computer Entertainment America LLC. Developed by thatgamecompany.

FIGURE 12.3 Jenova Chen, Kellee Santiago, *Flower*, 2007, video game for SONY PS3.
Source: Smithsonian American Art Museum. © 2008 Sony Computer Entertainment American LLC. Flower is a registered trademark of Sony Computer Entertainment America LLC. Developed by thatgamecompany.

from the visual arts and other types of digital media (Baptiste, 2013). Participating in an aesthetic discussion about video games as art, students will answer the following:

- Is *Flower* art? Are all video games art? What qualities make video games art or not art?
- What role does beauty play in art and game design?
- How did Chen and Santiago's idea development and wonderment shape *Flower*'s production?
- In aesthetics, institutionalism refers to experts in the art world—including museums—identifying what is art and not art and what belongs in museum collections (Dickie, 1974). In your opinion, why would museums choose to add video games to their collections?

STEAM AMPLIFIERS CHOICE #3—GAMING MUSIC AND EMOTION

Music was essential to produce the emotional responses that Chen and Santiago desired for *Flower* (Figure 12.4). They

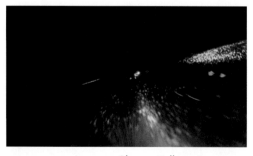

FIGURE 12.4 Jenova Chen, Kellee Santiago, *Flower*, 2007, video game for SONY PS3.
Source: Smithsonian American Art Museum. © 2008 Sony Computer Entertainment American LLC. Flower is a registered trademark of Sony Computer Entertainment America LLC. Developed by thatgamecompany.

commissioned composer and game audio designer Vicente Diamante early in the game's preproduction so that their team could have a guiding melody that defined *Flower*'s emotional tone (Innovation Stuntmen, 2010). Diamante played *Flower* during preproduction to understand it and explained: "I was also meditating, internalizing the rhythm, shape, and color of the world" (Lowe, para. 3). Through this process, he connected particular sounds to flower colors and suggested changes to the placement of flowers within the game so that the musical composition would match the visuals and desired emotions (Jeriaska, 2009). He selected instruments to present the flowers' perspectives:

> I really enjoyed taking some of the lower instruments, like bass flute and bassoon, and pushing them up into the higher registers, as opposed to using instruments like the piccolo or violin to convey the sense of flying through the air. These are flowers that are dreaming of flight: they are used to being down low, and in this game they are finally given opportunity to fly in these different environments.
>
> (Jeriaska, 2009)

Using Diamante's descriptions of his development processes for *Flower*, an analysis of the game's music during gameplay or through video clips, and a comparison of instruments including the bass flute, bassoon, piccolo, and violin, students can answer the National Core Music Standards #MU:Re8.1 Essential Question "How do we discern the musical creators' and performers' expressive intent?"

STEAM AMPLIFIERS CHOICE #4—ENGINEERING WIND TURBINES

Flower's wind turbines present a source of renewable energy for people to live in harmony with nature (Figure 12.5). A **wind turbine** converts the wind's kinetic rotation energy into electrical energy. The sun produces the **wind**—the natural movement of air molecules—by heating the Earth's land and water surfaces at uneven rates forming air pressure imbalances. Wind results when the warm air rises and colder air fills the spaces the warm air occupied. Meteorologists and engineers measure the wind by its direction and speed. Areas that produce large amounts of wind can be ideal sites to develop **wind farms** that consist of multiple wind turbines.

Mechanical engineers optimize wind turbine designs to produce the most efficient and cost-effective output. Horizontal-axis wind turbines are the most common. Their tall vertical monopole shafts place them at greater heights to harness more wind power. Designs with three blades produce the greatest efficiency because they weigh less and produce less drag. Their blades' teardrop forms resemble airplane propellers with aerodynamic designs that engineers set at the most efficient angles for rotation. **Wind vanes** identify the wind's direction and rotate the blades to access optimal wind force resistance. The wind turbine's **generator** converts the wind's kinetic energy and transfers it to the wind turbine's base. The wind farm's turbines are wired and divert their energy to a common **transformer**. Their energy is directed to a **substation** and produces the voltage needed to move to the transmission lines and electricity grids that power schools, homes, and businesses.

Students can develop fact sheets about wind turbines. Using brief, concise text, they will emphasize key vocabulary and can incorporate icons as teaching tools. Ideas for their fact sheets include (a) the parts of a wind turbine; (b) ways that wind turbines have become more efficient; (c) the steps engineers take to protect wildlife including birds, bats, and insects; (d) plans to reduce noise emissions; and (e) ideal locations to develop wind farms. They can augment learning by constructing a model wind turbine (Figure 12.6).

FIGURE 12.5 Jenova Chen, Kellee Santiago, *Flower*, 2007, video game for SONY PS3.

Source: Smithsonian American Art Museum. © 2008 Sony Computer Entertainment American LLC. Flower is a registered trademark of Sony Computer Entertainment America LLC. Developed by thatgamecompany.

FIGURE 12.6 High school students construct a model wind turbine.

Source: Photo by Allison Shelley/The Verbatim Agency for EDUimages. (CC BY-NC 4.0).

MOVING FULL STEAM AHEAD...

Jenova Chen and Kellee Santiago created *Flower* as an innovative video game that is also art. They shaped people's emotions through color, sounds, and movements that spark players' imaginations and wonderment as they journey through the game. In the next chapter, we will learn about Janet Echelman and how her installations spark people's imaginations and wonderment through lighting and movement.

References

Baptiste, L. (2013, December 17). *Smithsonian American Art Museum acquires video games.* Smithsonian. https://www.si.edu/newsdesk/releases/smithsonian-american-art-museum-acquires-video-games

Dickie, G. (1974). *Art and the aesthetic: An institutional analysis.* Cornell University Press.

Dugan, P. (2010, January 26). *Interview: ThatGameCompany's Santiago, Hunicke, on designing for the love.* Game Developer. https://www.gamasutra.com/view/news/26910/Interview_Thatgamecompanys_Santiago_Hunicke_On_Designing_For_The_Love.php

Field Level Media (2020, May 11). *Report: Gaming revenue to top $159B in 2020.* Reuters. https://www.reuters.com/article/esports-business-gaming-revenues/report-gaming-revenue-to-top-159b-in-2020-idUSFLM8jkJMl

Hour of Code. (2022). *Hour of Code activities.* https://hourofcode.com/us/learn

Innovation Stuntmen (2010, July 10). *Dopamin statt adrenalin: Der sensationelle erfolg von thatgamecompany.* Innovation Stuntmen. https://web.archive.org/web/20110503210602/http://www.innovationstuntmen.com/?p=526

Jeriaska (2009, February, 27). *Interview: A beautiful flight—Creating the music for Flower.* Gamasutra. https://www.gamasutra.com/view/news/22454/Interview_A_Beautiful_Flight__Creating_The_Music_For_Flower.php

Kumar, M. (2009, July 15). *Develop 2009: Thatgamecompany's Chen on how emotion can evolve games.* Gamasutra. https://www.gamasutra.com/view/news/24442/Develop_2009_Thatgamecompanys_Chen_On_How_Emotion_Can_Evolve_Games.php

Samyn, M. (2008, April). *Interview with Jenova Chen.* Tale of Tales. https://web.archive.org/web/20210414040405/http://tale-of-tales.com/blog/interviews/interview-with-jenova-chen/

Smithsonian American Art Museum. (2012, March 9). *"The Art of Video Games" interview with Kellee Santiago, Jenova Chen, and Robin Hunicke.* https://americanart.si.edu/videos/art-video-games-interview-kellee-santiago-jenova-chen-and-robin-hunicke-154287

Chapter 13

Janet Echelman

Illuminating the Built Environment

FIGURE 13.1 Janet Echelman, *1.8 Renwick*, 2015, knotted and braided fiber with programmable lighting above printed textile flooring.
Source: Smithsonian American Art Museum. © Janet Echelman.

Janet Echelman creates volumetric art installations formed from high-tech netting, some of which are 15 times stronger than steel by weight. Her airy installations move gracefully in the wind. As interactive designs, they encourage wonderment as audiences experience their changing colors and forms in motion (Smee, 2019). Echelman focuses on what she wants her art to become rather than concerning herself with obstacles that can arise from designing complex projects. Identifying her art as a collaborative effort, Echelman's team of experts includes engineers, architects, computer scientists, and lighting designers who bring her imaginative ideas to life.

Echelman even had specialized software developed to produce her installations:

> It's allowed me to explore density, shape, and scale with the forces of gravity and wind—all within the context of the built environment. We can manipulate designs and see the results immediately. It's transformed my process. I couldn't create what I do now without it.
>
> (Tucker, 2015)

Echelman utilizes scientifically-engineered twine and rope fibers that withstand environmental stressors, including hurricane-force winds, harsh ultraviolet

DOI: 10.4324/9781003183693-17

rays, and ice. Based on the handmade and digital models Echelman and her team create, industrial braiding and looming factories manufacture the vast quantities of netting that her sculptures require and then hand trim and knot the netted panels to replicate the look of age-old crafting traditions (Smee, 2019). The draped and layered netting form produces a transparent and luminous feel.

Echelman (2022) generated the idea to use fishnet as art when she participated in a Fulbright Senior Lectureship in India. Her paints had not arrived in the mail, and she needed an alternative medium to prepare for an exhibition. Watching local fishermen, she perceived their nets as sculptural forms and collaborated with them to produce the artworks she needed. This experience changed her artistic direction and demonstrated that through imagination and problem solving she could create previously unimaginable works.

1.8 Renwick presents Echelman's response to the 2011 Japanese Tohoku earthquake's powerful force that redistributed the earth's mass, shifted the position of its axis, changed its rotation, and shortened the day by 1.8 millionths of a second (Figure 13.1; Smee, 2020).

Echelman utilized recorded data from the National Oceanic and Atmospheric Administration and NASA about the earthquake and resulting tsunami to create her designs (Harvey, 2015). LED lights programmed in 30-minute sequences enhance *1.8 Renwick's* beauty and changing perceptions. Lavender and soft yellow-green colors flow onto the walls transforming them into a painted canvas that compliments the netting's golden yellows, orange, and purple hues. At other moments, the artwork's netted core glows like the morning sun and then fades into a deep sunset. Rich reds and fuchsias later saturate the room giving the feeling of jubilance. These radiating sequences of light cast shadows and unify the suspended sculpture with the 4,000 square-foot carpet beneath it made from netting materials that replicate the sea floor's topographical patterning produced by the tsunami (Harvey, 2015).

Teaching and Learning in the STEAM Artist's Studio 13.1 teaches about Echelman and her interactive installations. Its *STEAM Amplifiers* augment the lesson with content on sustainable-urban design, materials science and engineering, LED lighting, and aesthetic categories.

Teaching and Learning in the STEAM Artist's Studio 13.1

Introduce Janet Echelman and the importance of planning and communicating with clients and other stakeholders when creating interactive installations. Describe how Echelman makes sketches, creates miniature models, and uses three-dimensional computer models to form sculptures that have accurate proportions and billow with the wind.

Essential/Guiding Questions

1. Janet Echelman uses her imagination and wonderment to envision what her installations can become. Why is the artistic behavior of imagination and wonderment important to her planning process?
2. Echelman explained: "I might sketch 25 versions of an idea until it stops being an object to look at and becomes someplace I want to get lost in" (Smee, 2019). What qualities make people want to get lost in Echelman's installations?

Daily Learning Targets

As a design team, we can imagine and create an interactive art experience by modifying an actual space and/or forming a model.

- We can articulate the purpose and meanings of our interactive design.
- We can develop a clear plan of how people would interact with the space we designed.
- We can choose diverse media, including non-traditional media like repurposed netting and fabric, to produce our design.

National Core Arts Anchor Standards NVAS 1, 6, 8, and 11.
www.nationalartsstandards.org

Teaching for Students' Development

PK-12: (A) Ask students to identify the materials Echelman uses to create interactive installations and analyze their lighting changes and movements. (B) Explain how working in teams allows artists to achieve results that would be unattainable if working alone.

   Early childhood: Young children are inspired by play and explorative experiences that stimulate their cognitive development. Invite students to act out the movements of Echelman's installations.

   Middle childhood: Students can make predictions about how weather conditions like the wind influence the movements and appearances of Echelman's outdoor installations. Use class discussions and journals for students to articulate their thoughts.

   Early adolescence: Middle school students have developed greater abilities to represent three-dimensional spaces in their art. Ask students to describe the qualities of Echelman's volumetric forms and make a sketch that demonstrates how her art shows volume.

   Adolescence: High school students talk and write about art using technical vocabulary. Have students research and describe some of the technical innovations that drive Echelman's art installations.

STEAM AMPLIFIERS CHOICE #1—SUSTAINABLE URBAN DESIGN

Sustainable urban planning refers to the planning, development, management, and use of land in cities, towns, suburbs, and rural areas using environmentally sustainable materials and practices. As an interdisciplinary field, sustainable urban planning involves teams of experts that include architects, landscape architects, city planners, traffic engineers, environmental planners, and artists. The need for sustainable urban planning has increased with more people moving to urban environments. Urban planners form comprehensive plans regarding land usage, conservation, and social and economic sustainability while recognizing that communities best meet the needs of all people when they are inclusive, accessible, promote equity, and minimize humanity's imprint on the world. Urban designers meet with local planning authorities, citizens, and other stakeholders to learn their needs and work through possible constraints. Their designs incorporate plans to construct green buildings, replenish resources, use renewable energies and water sources, and protect living organisms. Sustainable urban development improves a community's health by providing access to green spaces, safe pedestrian zones and bike paths, and public transportation. Urban designers create mix-use spaces that reduce travel, as people can live, work, shop, and enjoy leisurely activities within close vicinities. Their designs include community centers and the arts. They plan for future growth and develop infrastructure strategies that foster community vibrancy and prevent the environmental degradation that arises when communities lack necessary resources.

FIGURE 13.2 Janet Echelman's *Bending Arc,* 2020, is an innovative installation that enhances the St. Pete Pier with its beauty, meaning, and wonderment.
Source: © Janet Echelman.

Urban designers identify a community's key locations, such as historic landmarks and natural spaces, to bring people together. Echelman designed *Bending Arc* (Figure 13.2), an installation on permanent display at the Pier District in St. Petersburg, Florida, which includes a museum, playground, beach, and solar car canopies that generate solar energy, reduce greenhouse gas emissions, and shade parked vehicles. *Bending Arc's* blue-and white-hued netting compliments the Florida sky during the day and glows bright fuchsia at night (Figure 13.3). Its title was inspired by Martin Luther King's speech that quoted abolitionist

FIGURE 13.3 Janet Echelman's *Bending Arc,* 2020, glows at night with bright fuchsia colors.
Source: © Janet Echelman.

Theodore Parker's statement "the arc of the moral universe is long, but it bends towards justice" (Smith, 2020). Echelman selected the quote in reference to the 1950s Supreme Court decision Alsup v. St. Petersburg that granted black community members equal access to segregated public pools. Echelman noted how *Bending Arc's* fluidity aligns with positive change and debuted during the George Floyd protests and calls for racial justice and civil rights for black and brown people: "I've been working on this piece for four years And I never would have guessed when the piece opened, it would open in such a pivotal time for social justice" (Smith, 2020).

FIGURE 13.4 Advanced materials enable Janet Echelman's installations to withstand various outdoor weather conditions. *As If It Were Already Here*, 2015, Boston.
Source: Studio Echelman, Photo: Bruce Petschek. (CC BY-SA 4.0), Wikimedia Commons.

STEAM AMPLIFIERS CHOICE #2—MATERIAL SCIENCE AND ENGINEERING

Materials science and engineering refers to the production and refinement of solid materials for industrial and personal use. It is an interdisciplinary field grounded in physics, chemistry, and engineering with the aim of making advanced materials from metals, ceramics, polymers, and composites (the combination of at least two different materials). Scientists and engineers study the properties and structures of materials, their relationships, and how they can be combined and processed to produce desired outcomes, including making new materials and improving existing ones so that they are lighter, smaller, stronger, and/or more cost-effective.

Advances in materials science and engineering have benefitted Echelman's work as she was able to substitute regular fishnet with stronger and lighter fibers, including a fiber created for NASA, to produce

larger sculptures that could withstand diverse weather conditions (Figure 13.4; Tucker, 2015). Studying materials science and engineering, students can also make connections to **nanotechnologies,** technologies that consist of tiny, lightweight parts—ones that make their mobile devices small and lightweight. They can investigate how humans have used metals and their applications in art. **Metallurgy** is the study of extracted metals and how they are modified for expanded uses. Students can examine how people combine metal with other metals and/or additional materials, such as silica and carbon, called **alloys**, to produce new metals.

STEAM AMPLIFIERS CHOICE #3—LED LIGHTING UP OUR LIVES

Lighting technologies have drastically changed since Thomas Edison's production of incandescent lightbulbs (see Chapter 2). Many people have switched to LED (light-emitting diode) lights due to their high-energy efficiency rates and cost savings. LED lighting is produced when an electrical current, consisting of charged electrons and holes, passes through a solid diode semiconductor. A **semiconductor** is an electronic conductivity material produced with an insulator and metal conductors. LED lights come in many shapes, sizes, and colors. They play key roles in sustainable architecture, landscape design, the arts, and brighten everyday objects including computers, mobile devices, and traffic lights. *1.8 Renick's* programmed LED lighting adds visual appeal with its fluctuating colors and moving shadows that interact with the artwork's 51 miles of high-tech twine (Figure 13.5).

Building on their studies, students can discuss how advances in LED lighting technologies resulted from developments in materials science and engineering. They can compare LED lights with incandescent lightbulbs and discover how LED lights are illuminated by electrons in a semiconductor and incandescent lightbulbs emit light from a glass vacuum. Metal filament warmed inside causes the lightbulb to illuminate. Ninety percent of the heat needed to illuminate incandescent lightbulbs is wasted. LED lights use 75% less energy than incandescent lightbulbs and thereby reduce greenhouse gas emissions. LED lights save consumers money because they use less energy and last approximately 25,000 hours compared to incandescent lightbulbs that last only 1,000 hours.

STEAM AMPLIFIERS CHOICE #4—AESTHETIC CATEGORIES

Echelman's web page (2022) explains that "Echelman's work defies categorization, as it intersects Sculpture, Architecture, Urban Design, Material Science, Structural & Aeronautical Engineering, and Computer Science." This statement holds true for Echelman's transdisciplinary approach to design. Students can also learn how **aestheticians**, philosophers of art, categorize art using criteria. **Mimesis** is the aesthetic category that values art that looks realistic and/or ideal. **Formalism** focuses on an artist's proficient design skills using the elements and principles of art and applications of art media. **Expressionism**

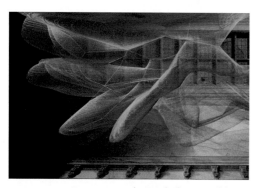

FIGURE 13.5 Programmed LED lighting adds to *1.8 Renwick's* aesthetic appeal.
Source: Smithsonian American Art Museum. © Janet Echelman.

FIGURE 13.6 Janet Echelman's conceptual design for *1.8 Renwick* invokes audiences' emotional responses as it teaches about environmental phenomena.
Source: Smithsonian American Art Museum. © Janet Echelman.

appraises art for its ability to communicate emotions through its subject matter and/or an artist's expressive media applications. **Contextualism** centers on the stories and meanings that drive artworks, as related to social, historic, ethical, and/or political perspectives. **Instrumentalism**, an outgrowth of contextualism, identifies how artists produce artworks for purposes beyond artworks, with emphasis on content relating to social, gender, ethnic, religious, and/or political issues.

Students will learn that an individual artwork can be examined using one or more categories (Sickler-Voigt, 2020). For example, students can refer to conceptualism to discuss Echelman's ideas for using netting and lighting to create volumetric sculptures that change the dynamics of built environment spaces (Figure 13.6). Expressionism applies to Echelman's ability to produce emotional responses to her artworks given their fluctuating movements and harmonious and vibrant colors. Instrumentalism applies to Echelman's designs. *1.8 Renick* teaches about humanity's interconnections to the earth and its powerful forces. *Bending Arc* takes actions against discriminatory practices.

MOVING FULL STEAM AHEAD...

This chapter on Janet Echelman described her imaginative ideas for designing art installations using innovative materials in built environment spaces. It concludes Part IV of this book with its emphasis on the artistic behavior of imagination and wonderment. In the next chapter, we will learn about graphic designer Litha Soyizwapi and his acclaimed *GauRider app*. It begins Part V of this book that focuses on the artistic behavior of persistence.

References

Echelman, J. (2022). *Janet Echelman biography.* Janet Echelman https://www.echelman.com/about

Harvey, L. (2015, November 20). How one artist learned to sculpt the wind. *Smithsonian.* https://www.smithsonianmag.com/smithsonian-institution/how-one-artist-learned-sculpt-wind-180957064/

Sickler-Voigt, D. C. (2020). *Teaching and learning in art education: Cultivating students' potential from pre-K through high school.* Routledge.

Smee, S. (2019, April 04). In the studio with Janet Echelman. *The Washington Post.* https://www.washingtonpost.com/graphics/2019/entertainment/in-the-studio-with-artist-janet-echelman/

Smee, S. (2020, January 31). A hugely popular hit returns to the Renwick. *The Washington Post.* https://www.washingtonpost.com/entertainment/museums/a-hugely-popular-hit-returns-to-the-renwick/2020/01/30/8c5d9720-3d35-11ea-b90d-5652806c3b3a_story.html

Smith, L. (2020, July 20). This new aerial sculpture in Florida is gorgeous. It's also a haunting reminder of an ugly past. *Fast Company.* https://www.fastcompany.com/90529220/this-new-aerial-sculpture-in-florida-is-gorgeous-its-also-a-haunting-reminder-of-an-ugly-past

Tucker, D. (2015, Spring/Summer). Discovering the unknown: An interview with Janet Echelman. *Public Art Review, 26*(2), 42–49.

PART V

Artists' Lessons to Thrive!
Persistence

Chapter 14

Litha Soyizwapi

Designing a Train of Thought

FIGURE 14.1 Litha Soyizwapi. *GauRider App Icon.* 2016.
Source: © Litha Soyizwapi.

The idiom train of thought accurately describes the sequencing of events that artist and designer Litha Soyizwapi applies to make decisions, solve problems, and reach effective outcomes to develop apps and create products his clients desire. Soyizwapi works through design challenges by applying creative thinking skills, asking why, and seeing things from multiple perspectives. Understanding his persistence and thought processes provides insights into the events, mindsets, and even failures that stimulate his professional practices.

Trained as a graphic designer, Soyizwapi is a self-taught app designer who has received international acclaim for his development of the *GauRider app* that makes commuting easier for passengers using the Gautrain rapid commuter rail and bus service in Gauteng, South Africa (Figures 14.1 and 14.2). A Gautrain user himself, Soyizwapi wanted to develop a more-efficient app than the ones that were

DOI: 10.4324/9781003183693-19

FIGURE 14.2 Litha Soyizwapi. *GauRider App* screen on an iPad.
Source: © Litha Soyizwapi.

available. He talked to commuters at train and bus stations to learn their needs and showed them working models of his app to improve its interface and user experience. Based on their responses and his own reflections, Soyizwapi designed the *GauRider app's* convenient drag-and-drop navigation feature that can be used offline to simplify commuters' abilities to access travel times and check their available balances. The *GauRider app* became South Africa's number one paid travel app for iPhone. Its success is due to Soyizwapi's thorough analysis of commuters' needs and knowledge of design technologies.

As a general rule, Soyizwapi asks why to create purposeful products that people want to use. He explained "why is the most important step in trying to solve any problem" and that additional questions follow (personal communication, 2021). Soyizwapi is persistent in exploring his subject matter in depth. He thinks about ideas and content from multiple perspectives to develop better solutions and fresh ideas. His quest to know more began in childhood with access to maps, books, atlases, and outdoor learning. During family road trips, Soyizwapi's mother, a geography

teacher, showed him river formations and meanderings. He reflected: "This taught me to observe. I also learnt that all things are one. Every single thing is part of a whole. This is true for design and programming" (personal communication, 2021).

Clients commission Soyizwapi to produce effective branding and design products. During consultations, clients discover that Soyizwapi's creative process differs from the general practices of advertising and marketing departments that focus solely on designs and messages. Soyizwapi invests time and patience to understand how each company operates. He talks to company owners and CEOs to learn about their businesses from the ground up. Soyizwapi reviews companies' financial statements, learns board members' interests, and identifies what motivates employees. He explained: "Everyone chips in. Everyone is represented. They get a sense of ownership" (personal communication, 2021). By learning all aspects of each business and its people, Soyizwapi becomes a trusted and equal collaborator.

Final designs begin after Soyizwapi has secured background information, identified clients' goals, and recognized the problems, constraints, and solutions. His knowledge of aesthetic design brings his clients' ideas to life:

> It makes me … a better curator, to edit things out and communicate what is important at a particular time. It helps me to define the focal point of the overall composition, to use the best typography, layout, imagery, iconography or animation. The visual polish makes the solution delightful, surprising and memorable.
>
> (personal communication, 2021)

Soyizwapi recommends that others follow his lead in valuing the creative process, taking their time, and evolving their work by showing up each day. He augments his ideas by working through the challenges that can result from trying something ambitious and learning emerging technologies.

Like a spectacular train ride that reaches its final destination, people take notice of Soyizwapi's designs and comment "Wow, this is great!" They want more. Soyizwapi's quality outcomes and word of mouth secure him additional clients. He begins the process of laying fresh tracks to start his next creative and inclusive journey. All are welcome aboard!

Presenting *Teaching and Learning in the STEAM Artist's Studio 14.1*, we will describe how Soyizwapi's persistence in

---

Teaching and Learning in the STEAM Artist's Studio 14.1

Introduce students to Litha Soyizwapi and discuss how his *Gaurider app* fulfills a need. Ask students to describe how apps are computer programs and identify their purposes. Throughout their app's development, have students document their creative growth; explain how all participants cultivated shared ownership of the project; and, identify the constraints and challenges they experienced.

Essential/Guiding Questions

1. How does Soyizwapi's thinking process—his train of thought—influence the products he creates?
2. What roles do persistence, collaboration, and problem-solving play in Soyizwapi's idea development?

Daily Learning Targets

As designers, we can design an app based on a need and make revisions to improve its design. (Our design can be in the form of sketches with written descriptions of its uses that can progress into an actual app.)

- We can design an app logo using drawing, painting, or digital media that represents our app.
- We can plan how users will interact with our app and outline its design qualities.

- We can design an app using a programming environment, such as Code.org's App Lab.
- We can describe our selected need and how our app satisfies that need.

National Core Arts Anchor Standards NVAS 3, 5, 8, and 11.
www.nationalartsstandards.org

Teaching for Students' Development

PK-12: (A) Have students discuss how persistence and a train of thought represent the steps people make to reach conclusions, like Soyizwapi did to create the *GauRider app*. (B) Ask students to explain how designing an app requires many steps and problem-solving.

Early childhood: Young children can make connections between existing and new knowledge. Ask students to describe what an app is and provide examples of ones they know. Break down key vocabulary using terms students know and make connections to their experiences, such as when they make art on a tablet, they are using an app. Introduce programs such as Code.org's CS Fundamentals for app design and provide close guidance as they work.

Middle childhood: Students' cognitive development has expanded their concrete reasoning skills, and they are starting to think abstractly. Discuss ways for students to include symbols and abstractions to convey meaning. Utilize program such as Code.org's CS Fundamentals and assist students as they create their apps.

Early adolescence: Students are augmenting their deductive reasoning skills. With a focus on client needs and existing constraints, students can apply creative means to produce a final solution through app design. Introduce programs such as Code.org's CS Discoveries for middle school students and App Lab that is designed for ages 13+.

Adolescence: Students are able to contemplate multiple possibilities to solve particular situations. Based on their choices, they will present multiple ideas to guide clients' selections. Utilize programs such as Code.org's CS Discoveries for high school students and App Lab.

learning new skills including app design and his keen interest in hearing people's ideas have made him a highly proficient and sought-after artist and designer. The *STEAM Amplifiers* describe user experience and user interface design, app design, sustainable transportation, and thriving through failures.

STEAM AMPLIFIERS CHOICE #1—USER EXPERIENCE AND USER INTERFACE DESIGN

Bringing **systems** to life, including websites, apps, and computer programs, involves effective planning and design of the **user experience** (UX) and **user** interface (UI). UX refers to the interactions between human users and a system. UX designers plan the system's general concepts and design a skeletal structure that outlines its basic content and navigational flow. They mitigate technical errors to alleviate negative experiences and possible barriers. Designers build upon the UX designs to develop the UI design through their careful selection of color schemes, typography, visual images, and navigation buttons. A harmonious relationship results when the UX and UI are easy to navigate, stimulate the senses, serve users' needs, and are fully functional.

International Organization for Standardization (ISO) (2018) defined **usability** as: "the extent to which a system, product or service can be used by specified users to achieve specified goals with effectiveness, efficiency and satisfaction in a specified context of use" (Introduction, para 2). Effective system designs are intuitive, quick, accurate, and consistent. **Human-centered design** has added values because they encourage developers and designers to place emphasis on people's personal needs that include physical comfort through ergonomic designs and accessibility so that people with varying abilities can operate systems independently.

Students can explore UX and UI design by analyzing age-appropriate apps and their designs. They can make a note of the apps' structures, key features, targeted ages, design style, and navigation and performance tools. For example, users of the *GauRider* app value its drag-and-drop navigation feature (Figure 14.2) and its ability to work offline. Students can numerically rank the effectiveness of the visual designs, usability, and accessibility of the apps they have studied with number one being the most successful.

STEAM AMPLIFIERS CHOICE #2—APP DESIGN

People download apps 700 million times each day from platforms such as iOS and Android. App categories include social networking, entertainment, education, games, and travel—such as Soyizwapi's *GauRider app* (Figure 14.3). With society's increasing demands for apps, students are learning app design as part of their studies. Programs, such as Code.org's App Lab, simplify learning app design basics with helpful visual tutorials, animated gifs that illustrate steps to complete tasks, and teacher instructional resources. In App Lab, users have a designated workspace for designing and coding and can preview their app's screen appearance and operations. App Lab uses JavaScript as its programming language—with students having the options of designing with written code and blocks of code. Its **design toolbox** feature provides functional elements for students to design the app's multiple screens with images, canvases for drawing, and written labels, as well as interactive user tools that

FIGURE 14.3 Litha Soyizwapi. *GauRider App's* design welcomes riders on board GauTrain. *Source: © Litha Soyizwapi.*

include buttons, text input, dropdowns, sliders, and checkboxes. Students can create original components and choose from integrated design color themes. The tutorials and guided practice assist students in developing skills so that they can work toward creating more complex and innovative designs.

STEAM AMPLIFIERS CHOICE #3—SUSTAINABLE TRANSPORTATION

Gautrain (2018) is a form of sustainable public transportation. Its train and bus services are sustainable because they are designed to "meet the needs of the present generation without compromising the ability of future generations to meet their own needs" (para. 3; Figure 14.4). Serving the masses, Gautrain reduces greenhouse emissions, traffic, automobile accidents, and noise pollution because people do not need to rely solely on personal automobiles to get where they need to go. The United Nations (2015) has set goals to expand sustainable public transportation, like Gautrain, and "provide access to safe, affordable, accessible and sustainable transport systems for all…" (Goal 11.2). As part of this plan, the goals addressed the need to pay "special attention to the needs of those in vulnerable situations, women, children, persons with disabilities and older persons" (Goal 11.2). Gautrain has aligned with the United Nations' goal and made its transportation services accessible and more affordable. Gautrain's approach to transportation links societal, economic, and environmental needs. It recognizes that access to mobility facilitates job production and thereby helps improve people's standards of living.

FIGURE 14.4 Inspired by Gautrain and the *GauRider* app, this tunnel book's sculpted train reinforces the need for sustainable transportation.

Source: © Debrah Sickler-Voigt, Paige Brenner, and Richard Sickler. Photo: Richard Sickler.

Reflecting on the United Nations' goal to make transportation sustainable and more accessible to people, students will take an inventory of public transportation in their own communities and answer guiding questions to facilitate their studies: "Is there adequate public transportation in our community?" Who does it serve? Is it meeting the needs of the community? What works well? How can it be improved? Students can expand their study of sustainable transportation to investigate access to safe bike paths and walkways for pedestrians. They can look to resources such as transportation specialists, routes, maps, and satellite images to aid their studies.

STEAM AMPLIFIERS CHOICE #4—THRIVING THROUGH FAILURES

During a TEDx Talk, Litha Soyizwapi stated "My story is a story of failure. It is a story of gaining confidence and a story of achieving relative success" (TEDxTalks, 2014; Figure 14.5). He explained his struggles learning drawing in college and teaching himself coding. Soyizwapi wanted to share his failures because he noticed that people will openly discuss their failures and frustrations in ordinary conversations; however, they rarely speak about their failures in formal presentations. He further explained that "creation is messy" and "things take time to grasp

FIGURE 14.5 Litha Soyizwapi talks about his struggles and failures as an artist and designer to help others.
Source: Photo: Victor Dlamini.

and understand" (personal communication, 2021). At times when people lose their energy and motivation, Soyizwapi believes people need passion and love for what they do to carry them forward.

When researching the benefits of failures in science, Firestein (2016), identified how schoolchildren seldomly learn about failure in textbooks filled with examples of final results. Firestein prefers teaching students science in context so that they learn about inventions' development and not just study final results. Scientific inventions including penicillin, X-ray machines, and Post-it notes all resulted from mistakes. Similarly, visual artists and designers progress through a series of processes to produce end results to generate ideas and discover creative solutions. Given artists' and scientific examples, students will discuss how failure can spark new growth and foster resiliency. They will use journals, photographs of in-progress works, and critiques to document their creative processes and identify how they worked through failures and can recognize failure as a normal part of the human experience.

MOVING FULL STEAM AHEAD...

Graphic designer Litha Soyizwapi created his *GauRider app* to meet people's needs. Through his persistence and desire to know more, Soyizwapi acquired available resources to teach himself app design and coding. He works through failures to reach his goals. We gained knowledge of user experience and user interface design, app design, and sustainable transportation. In the next chapter, we will study Jim Henson and how his persistence and beliefs in his Muppets led to their global success.

References

Firestein, S. (2016). *Failure: Why science is so successful.* Oxford University Press.

Gautrain. (2018). *Gautrain—A sustainable development initiative.* https://web.archive.org/web/20210806004305/https://gma.gautrain.co.za/development/Pages/sustainable-development.aspx

International Organization for Standardization (ISO). 2018. *ISO 9241-11:2018(en): Ergonomics of human-system interaction—Part 11: Usability: Definitions and concepts.* https://www.iso.org/obp/ui/#iso:std:iso:9241:-11:ed-2:v1:en

TEDxTalks. (2014). *How I taught myself to code: Litha Soyizwapi at TEDxSoweto.* [video]. YouTube. https://www.youtube.com/watch?v=nmZR_JsLCfg

United Nations. (2015, October 21). *Transforming our world: The 2030 Agenda for Sustainable Development.* https://www.un.org/ga/search/view_doc.asp?symbol=A/RES/70/1&Lang=E

Chapter 15

Jim Henson

Big Leaps and So Much Laughter

FIGURE 15.1 Jim Henson. *Kermit the Frog.* Late 1970s.
Source: Division of Cultural and Community Life, National Museum of American History, Smithsonian Institution.

Jim Henson knew how to make people laugh by creating a world of puppets called Muppets—a term he coined in 1955 to differentiate his puppets from all others. Henson's puppetry skills were recognized in high school, and he received his first television show *Sam and Friends* (1955–61) in college. His creative works also included *Sesame Street* (launched in 1969), *The Muppet Show* (1976–81), *The Dark Crystal* (1982), *Fraggle Rock* (1983–87), and numerous movies and spinoffs. Henson's most recognizable Muppet, Kermit the Frog (Figure 15.1), first appeared on *Sam and*

DOI: 10.4324/9781003183693-20

Friends. Henson designed Kermit as a cross between a hand and a rod puppet using his mother's old coat, a pair of jeans, and a Ping-Pong ball cut in half for eyes. By creating his Muppets with soft materials, Henson could give them a broad array of facial and bodily expressions using hand gestures.

When Henson joined *Sesame Street*, he brought Kermit the Frog with him and created additional Muppet characters including Big Bird and Oscar the Grouch (Figure 2.2). By operating the Kermit Muppet and giving him his own voice, Henson fostered Kermit's wit and charm. One of Kermit's most memorable roles was working as a roving reporter for Sesame Street's *News Flash* segment (Connell et al., 1972–1989). Decked in a trench coat and fedora, Kermit carried a large microphone and traveled to numerous destinations asking pertinent questions, seeking the truth, and drawing conclusions—similar to the inquiry techniques that STEAM professionals use. His *News Flash* segments centering on fairytales, fables, nursery rhymes, and history were rife with educational content. Frequent mishaps occurred despite Kermit's serious reporting. When *News*

FIGURE 15.2 Kermit the Frog interviews Humpty Dumpty.

Source: Jim Henson, creator. Sesame Street YouTube Channel. "Sesame Street: Humpty Dumpty's Fall, Kermit News." Fair Use.

Flash went live on air, Kermit typically had his back to the camera and scrambled to utter "Hi ho, this is Kermit the Frog" to begin his report. To Kermit's frustration, his reports were parodies. When interviewing the nursery rhyme character Humpty Dumpty (Figure 15.2), who had just been put back together after a great fall, Kermit gave him a congratulatory pat on the back and said, "It's very nice to have you back." Kermit's gesture accidentally knocked Humpty Dumpty off the wall he was sitting on and necessitated that he be put back together all over again.

Recognizing the Muppets' appeal to people of all ages, Henson had the innovative idea of developing a prime-time variety show called *The Muppet Show*. Despite previous successes, television networks in the United States rejected his idea—thinking no one would watch. In his autobiography, *Kermit the Frog* (2006) recalled the negative responses, including: "We ABSOLUTELY LOVE the concept, EXCEPT for the part about its being a prime-time, big budget show featuring celebrity guest stars and a still-unknown cast of Muppets and other creatures" (p. 42). Based on his persistence and innovative approaches to entertainment, Henson convinced British producer Lew Grade to produce his show. Kermit the Frog was *The Muppet Show's* protagonist among a cast of Muppets. It became an international success broadcasted in over 100 countries and received up to 235 million weekly viewers.

In remembering Henson, who passed away in 1990, Bonnie Erickson (Olson, 2014), the executive director of The Jim Henson Legacy, explained:

> He was persistent: there were many times that ideas he had did not succeed, but they would survive to live

again later.... I hope that kind of persistence and belief in himself is something that translates to everyone who learns [*sic*] about his life and his work.

Henson made hard work, creative risks, and persistence look easy. His humorous performances and adlib lines have made learning fun for countless children and entertained people of all ages. His Muppets continue to have relevance.

In presenting *Teaching and Learning in the STEAM Artist's Studio 15.1*, we will reference Henson's persistence and teach students how to create a comedic STEAM news report. The *STEAM Amplifiers* describe the neuroscience of goal setting, the value of laughter, green scientific reporting, and financial literacy.

Teaching and Learning in the STEAM Artist's Studio 15.1

Teach students about Jim Henson and how he used persistence to achieve his Muppet dream. To prepare students to create their own comedic news report with original puppets, have them analyze Muppets' video clips featuring Kermit the Frog. Explain how Henson used television and film screens as dynamic alternatives to restrictive puppet stages. Henson utilized close-up camera angles to emphasize his Muppets' emotions and distinct personalities.

Essential/Guiding Questions

1. How did Henson's creativity and persistence benefit him in achieving his artistic vision?
2. Kermit the Frog took news reporting seriously. In your opinion, why would Henson choose to add humor to Kermit's *News Flash* segment? How can humor help people learn?

Daily Learning Targets

As a team, we can create a puppet production about a comedic news report on a STEAM topic.

- We can design original puppets using the media of our choice.
- We can write an original comedic news report script on a STEAM topic.
- We can conduct interviews like Kermit did.
- We can film our performance and use the camera screen as an alternative to a puppet stage.
- We can present our comedic news report that runs one-to-five minutes and is unified in its content and design.

National Core Arts Anchor Standards NVAS 2, 6, 8, and 11.
www.nationalartsstandards.org

Teaching for Students' Development

PK-12: (A) Discuss how persistence can help people achieve their goals. (B) Show students a sampling of Henson's Muppets and video clips of him performing with them. Demonstrate how to create different types of puppets. Simpler examples include paper bag puppets, cardstock puppets, spoon puppets, and paper plate puppets. Rod puppets, sewn fabric puppets, papier-mâché puppets, and marionettes are more complex.

Early childhood: Young children build communication skills by asking questions and through hands-on learning. Have students focus on a STEAM topic and summarize ideas to determine how they can act out what they have learned using a puppet and by developing a script.

Middle childhood: Students are learning about news literacy and are beginning to determine if news stories are fact-based and credible. Have students read and watch age-appropriate news reports on STEAM topics to identify credible facts as inspirations to drive their comedic news reports.

Early adolescence: Middle school students can identify how some news organizations overuse the term breaking news to bring attention to their programs. Ask students to identify authentic examples of breaking news in STEAM subjects and compare them to inauthentic news examples.

Adolescence: High school students need communication skills that prepare them for college and vocational careers. Teach students about news writing as a profession. News writers begin their stories with a **lede**, an introduction, that presents the most important information. Their reports should be understandable for audiences, answer important questions, and include facts, quotes, and reliable sources. As an extension of their studies, students could visit a broadcast studio to learn how they operate.

STEAM AMPLIFIERS CHOICE #1— *THE RAINBOW CONNECTION* AND NEUROSCIENCE

During the opening scene of *The Muppet Movie* (Frawley, 1979; Figure 15.3), Kermit the Frog sings the *Rainbow Connection* in a picturesque swamp. He contemplates his dreams, goals, and aspirations. Kermit's goal to leave the swamp, become famous, and make people happy is connected to **neuroscience**, the scientific study of the body's nervous system. Scientists use **neuroimaging research** (taking images of the

Someday we'll find it, the rainbow connection.

FIGURE 15.3 The Library of Congress' National Recording Registry recognized *The Rainbow Connection* song in 2020 for long-term preservation.
Source: The Muppet's YouTube channel. "Kermit the Frog Sing Along, Rainbow Connection, Muppets." Fair Use.

brain to identify activities) to study how the brain influences people's abilities to set goals and change behaviors. Prior negative experiences and social rejections can hinder people from reaching their goals. Berkman (2018) explained: "grounded in the neuroscience of motivation and reinforcement learning is to start behavior change with modest goals and reward even the smallest steps toward them" (p. 14). When people set goals that align with their identities, they are more likely to attain them. Applying persistence and having a support system builds people's resiliency as they work through struggles to achieve their goals. Such was the case with Jim Henson creating *The Muppet Show*. Kermit the Frog also reached his goal of being famous despite obstacles.

Our instruction can help students learn how to attain personally-driven goals that are broken down into manageable steps. We can share Henson's biography and reference Kermit's achievement of fame as presented in *The Muppet Movie* finale that shows the Muppets singing the *Rainbow Connection* and reinforcing viewers to keep believing and keep pretending because they did what they set out to do.

Jim would break down into a fit of his high-pitched giggles, laughing until tears ran down his face" (p. 161). Working together, they often improvised and knew how to make dull material exceptionally funny. Their laughter was contagious.

The Mayo Clinic (2021) described the benefits of laughter as a stress reliever. Laughter increases people's oxygen intake, which in return is also beneficial to the heart, lungs, and muscles. It increases endorphins, which are hormones, and stimulates circulation. People experience relaxation from elevating their heart rates from laughter and then gently decreasing their heart rates after their laughter has ended. Long-term benefits may include greater personal satisfaction, improved moods, less pain, and a better immune system. In addition to shared humor that comes from being around others (Figure 15.4), people can look to humorous materials—including Jim Henson's Muppets. Students can watch Jim Henson's Muppet performances and rank them according to how much they made them laugh, such as one meaning little or no laughter and five meaning hysterically-funny laughter. Students will also discuss ethics and how to be kind with their

STEAM AMPLIFIERS CHOICE #2—LAUGHTER IS CONTAGIOUS AND GOOD FOR US!

Henson's collaborator, Frank Oz, who operated Miss Piggy, Fozzie Bear, and Bert of Bert and Ernie (as well as Yoda for George Lucas) described how much he enjoyed performing with Henson and watching him laugh. Jones (2016), Henson's biographer, explained: "Jim [Henson] and Oz would get so wrapped up in their ad-libbing that

FIGURE 15.4 Third-grade students laugh and smile as they solve math problems.
Source: Photo by Allison Shelley/The Verbatim Agency for EDUimages. (CC BY-NC 4.0).

laughter making sure they are not harming and/or making fun of others.

STEAM AMPLIFIERS CHOICE #3—IT'S SO EASY BEIN' GREEN SCIENTIFIC REPORTING

Kermit the Frog is noticeably green. It is an important part of his identity. In the song "Bein' Green" written by Joe Raposo, Kermit initially thinks that his color is ordinary, but then realizes that many wonderful things in nature are green. His green identity eventually led to Kermit becoming the "spokesfrog" for a hybrid vehicle that showed Kermit enjoying the green outdoors by participating in sports that included mountain bike riding, kayaking, and rock climbing (AdAge, 2006). Kermit's physique serves as a visual cue for people to "go green" and make environmentally-responsible decisions to preserve the earth's natural resources. Using Kermit's example, students will identify green themes for a scientific report of their choosing. Examples may include natural spaces in their communities, solar power (Figure 15.5), wind power

(see Chapter 12), green algae as renewable energy, green architecture, and green technologies. Students can work in small groups or as a whole class for their scientific reporting. Their work can be a presentation of information or an experiment using the scientific method to test a hypothesis. They may choose to create models, displays, journals, charts, written reports, and/or a video to present their findings.

STEAM AMPLIFIERS CHOICE #4—IN THE GREEN: LEAPING INTO FINANCIAL LITERACY

In his biography, Kermit the Frog (2006) admitted to his own financial struggles—such as stashing cash between sofa cushions instead of using the bank—and offered his readers the financial success

FIGURE 15.5 High school students construct a solar-powered boat.

Source: Photo by Allison Shelley/The Verbatim Agency for EDUimages. (CC BY-NC 4.0).

FIGURE 15.6 Jim Henson (Artist) and Jerry Nelson (Performer) *Count von Count.* 1994.

Source: Puppet, Division of Cultural and Community Life, National Museum of American History, Smithsonian Institution.

strategies he learned. Being in the green refers to a person having a profitable and balanced budget compared to being in the red and having debt. It is necessary that students learn wise spending habits and understand like Kermit that money "does NOT grow on trees" (p. 100). Kermit's financial advice and his fellow Sesame Street character Count von Count's (Figure 15.6) love of counting can assist students in hopping into financial literacy.

One helpful resource is the Federal Deposit Insurance Corporation's (2022) Smart Money Program for grades Pre-K-12 that teaches students financial responsibility. It offers four curriculums with lesson plans and instructional resources for Grades Pre-K through 2; Grades 3–5; Grades 6–8; and Grades 9–12. Students can learn wise purchasing decisions, how to set financial goals, budgeting, price comparisons, and charitable giving—which Kermit warmheartedly advised "Our true worth is measured by what we give, not what we have" (p. 102).

MOVING FULL STEAM AHEAD...

In this chapter, we learned how Jim Henson's persistence brought his Muppets global acclaim and how he used humor to teach and entertain audiences, as seen with Kermit the Frog's reporting. We studied neuroscience, laughter's benefits, green scientific reporting, and financial literacy. In the next chapter, we will learn about paper engineer and book artist Sally Blakemore who has applied persistence to engineer innovative pop-up books.

References

AdAge. (2006, February 5). *Ford-easy being green.* https://adage.com/videos/ford-easy-being-green/605

Berkman, E. T. (2018). The neuroscience of goals and behavior change. *Consulting Psychology Journal, 70*(1), 28–44. doi: 10.1037/cpb0000094.

Connell, D., Stone, J., Hyslop, A., & Singer, D. (Executive Producers). (1972–1989). *Sesame Street, News Flash* [TV series]. Children's Television Network.

Federal Deposit Insurance Corporation. (2022, April 20). *Money smart for young people.* https://www.fdic.gov/resources/consumers/money-smart/teach-money-smart/money-smart-for-young-people/index.html

Frawley, J. (1979). *The Muppet Movie* [Film]. ICT Entertainment Henson Associates [Production Company].

Jones, B. J. (2016). *Jim Henson the biography.* Ballantine Books.

Kermit the Frog. (2006). *Before you leap: A frog eye's view of life's greatest lessons.* Disney.

Mayo Clinic. (2021, July 29). *Stress relief from laughter: It's no joke.* https://www.mayoclinic.org/healthy-lifestyle/stress-management/in-depth/stress-relief/art-20044456

Olson, P. (2014). *Ten questions with a Muppet maker: "Børk! Børk! Børk!"* National Museum of American History. https://americanhistory.si.edu/blog/2014/03/recently-a-new-group-of-puppets-went-on-view-in-ourpuppetry-in-americadisplay-intern-peter-olson-interviewed-bonnie-erickso.html

Chapter 16

Sally Blakemore

Engineering 360° Pop-Up Books

FIGURE 16.1 Sally Blakemore, *NASCAR Pop-Up Book: A Guide to the Sport,* The Hauler, 2009.
Source: Engineered by Sally Blakemore. Illustrated by Doug Chezem. Photo: Richard Sickler.

Good cheer abounds when award-winning paper artist Sally Blakemore creates books. As the owner of Arty Projects Studio, she has been commissioned to produce over 200 traditional flat and pop-up books for major publishing companies. Her resume is enriched with job titles that include paper engineer, author, creative director, and artistic production manager. In the early 1980s, Blakemore became fascinated with pop-up books. She learned how to create pop-ups by taking them apart and studying their structures and designs. Blakemore's persistent quest for knowledge about pop-up books continued, and she learned all aspects of packaging design from the earliest stages of idea development to final book production. A single mass-marketed book can take four years to produce with a team of 1,200 people.

The pop-up book pages Blakemore designs range from simple flaps, as represented in her celebrated book *Peek-A-Moo*, to intricate ones with dynamic three-dimensional pages, as seen in her *NASCAR Pop-Up Book: A Guide to The Sport* (Figure 16.1). Blakemore constructs pop-ups using **free-form paper engineering**. Instead of focusing on rulers and protractors to construct her designs, she follows her artistic intuitions and plays with paper folds to see where they want to go when opened as three-dimensional projections. She knows exactly how the paper will rip and to what extremes she can manipulate it into successfully engineered designs. She has a keen ability to visualize designs from multiple perspectives, which assists her in producing exhilarating book forms. Blakemore's pop-up forms include flaps

DOI: 10.4324/9781003183693-21

(see Figure 16.2's tailgate party), V-folds (see Figures 16.1–16.3's crowds), platform designs (Figures 16.2's barbecue grill), and pull-out tabs (Figure 16.2's NASCAR Sprint Cup Series Tracks).

Blakemore's book-engineering methods draw inspirations from her childhood due to dyslexia and synesthesia impacting how she learns and processes information. Blakemore did not learn how to read until age nine. To compensate, she went into dark rooms to mute the contrast of the black type and also tilted her books in many directions to process text more clearly (personal communication, 2022). **Dyslexia** is a neurobiological learning disability that causes difficulties with necessary word recognition, fluency, and accuracy for effective reading, writing, and spelling. People with dyslexia can also have the advantages of visualizing objects, memories, and fantasies from varying perspectives and with clear details. They can also develop superb reasoning and problem-solving skills. These qualities are highly beneficial in art and design (Sickler-Voigt, 2020). **Synesthesia** is a perceptual condition that joins the senses and produces automatic responses that alter a person's perceptions. Blakemore sees black-typed letters in red and green colors (Olmon, 2009). Synesthesia heightens synesthetes' visualization skills and is more prevalent in artists (Cytowic & Eagleman, 2011). Blakemore's childhood reading disability prompted her school to test her IQ. Students like Blakemore, who are gifted and talented and also have a disability, are referred to as **twice exceptional**. Reflecting on this diagnosis as an adult, Blakemore explained that her "gift is curiosity. It is what really taught me to read eventually, finding the thread and finding books that

FIGURE 16.2 Sally Blakemore, *NASCAR Pop-Up Book: A Guide to the Sport,* Blimp with Tailgate Party, 2009. This spread includes a simple flap, V-folds, a platform, and a pull-out tab. The flap on the far-left side enlarges the book spread when opened. Blakemore designed the crowds of people at the book's crease using V-folds. She engineered the pickup-truck bed using a raised platform that transforms into a BBQ grill when opened. The book's right-hand side contains a green pull-out tab with written information.
Source: Engineered by Sally Blakemore. Illustrated by Doug Chezem. Photo: Richard Sickler.

FIGURE 16.3 Sally Blakemore, *NASCAR Pop-Up Book: A Guide to the Sport,* Leaving the Track, 2009. This scene shows the backside of Blakemore's V-folds. The tabs support the figures' standing positions. Tabs are generally unnoticed in traditional book forms because they are on the unprinted backsides of pages. Due to Blakemore's 360° design, her tabs have been incorporated into the page illustrations.
Source: Engineered by Sally Blakemore. Illustrated by Doug Chezem. Photo: Richard Sickler.

complete the whole story" (personal communication, 2022). It also drives her art and ability to persist through challenges.

Blakemore (2017) advocates that children learn in ways that extend beyond testing—with which she struggled. Understanding that people process information differently, Blakemore engineers books in the round visible from 360° that invite book participants to examine text and images from various viewpoints. Participants want to turn her books in different directions to acquire information, as is the case with her NASCAR book that she wrote and engineered. Blakemore spent 10 hours in the pitstops taking in its sights, smells, and sounds to integrate the sport's sensory qualities in the book. She also invited her brother Paul R. Blakemore, a Grammy-winning audio engineer, to record a 12-second sound clip of the classic "Ladies and Gentlemen!" featuring an announcer's voice and race car engine sounds to give the impression of being at the racetrack. These qualities rev up book participants' minds and invite them to come back for more!

Teaching and Learning in the STEAM Artist's Studio 16.1 reinforces how

---

Teaching and Learning in the STEAM Artist's Studio 16.1

Introduce students to Sally Blakemore and describe how she used persistence to learn how to read and engineer pop-up books. Demonstrate how to create pop-ups beginning with simple flaps and V-folds. Explain how paper engineering fosters students' intuitive mathematical abilities because students learn mathematical skills as they learn how to fold paper to produce angled designs and then flatten and raise them to learn where the paper wants to go. Lastly, describe how Blakemore and her team of creators generate preliminary book ideas and produce **comps** (comprehensive models of pop-up pages and text) to present to publishers. Based on publisher feedback, Blakemore and her team make revisions and produce new comps. When the final comp is approved, it is sent off for printing and final production.

Essential/Guiding Questions

1. How did persistence and artistic intuition aid Blakemore in engineering pop-up books? Describe a time that you applied persistence to work through an obstacle.
2. Why does Blakemore engineer books from multiple perspectives?

Daily Learning Targets

As an artistic team, we can create a pop-up book.
- We can identify the best materials to design our books using inspirations from pop-up books we analyzed.
- We can write a narrative for our pop-up book.

- We can design a front cover with a title and a back cover that illustrates what our book is about.
- We can create at least four sets of interior pages, called the series, to present the book's story.
- We can refine and unify the pop-up book's images and text so that all parts belong together.

National Core Arts Anchor Standards NVAS 3, 5, 7, and 10.
www.nationalartsstandards.org

Teaching for Students' Development

PK-12: (A) Collect pop-up books from the library and/or build a collection of books so that students can examine their paper engineering structures and how complex designs consist of multiple parts. (B) Using the collection of pop-up books, ask students to identify the qualities that make them unified in their engineering designs, illustrations, and written narratives.

Early childhood: Young children can construct simple models. Teach students how to make pop-up folds, such as a flap, and describe the importance of the flap as a design solution that fits within the book when closed.

Middle childhood: Students can solve simple design problems. Demonstrate how to fold paper to create V-folds that fit within the students' pop-up book's forms.

Early adolescence: Middle school students can evaluate design solutions. Have students examine pop-up books to explain how their constructions resulted in effective designs. Teach students how to practice replicating and manipulating the books' pop-up forms to create original designs.

Adolescence: High school students can apply engineering skills to solve real-world problems. Have students work in teams to create more complex original folds that fit within their book's form and design a book that teaches about a relevant issue.

Blakemore applied persistence to overcome reading barriers and developed innovative ways to design pop-up books in the round. Its *STEAM Amplifiers* address the aerodynamics of safe travels, recipe measurements, sociology, and designing books to teach STEAM.

STEAM AMPLIFIERS CHOICE #1—SAFE AERODYNAMIC TRAVELS

NASCAR drivers reach speeds of 180+ mph/290+ km/h. Engineers design NASCAR vehicles with **aerodynamic** designs—meaning the air flow contours a race car's form so that it is faster and more fuel efficient. Drivers use the principles of **aerodynamics**—drag, downforce, and drafting—to their advantages. **Drag** is the air's resistance against a race car. The aerodynamic design reduces drag forces, so the race car drives faster. **Downforce** identifies how the air pushes the race car down and helps it grip the track. **Drafting** describes how two race cars—with one driving closely behind the other—create a pull that makes them both drive faster. Given racing's high speeds, NASCAR engineers utilize innovative technologies to keep drivers safe and minimize the damages of crashes (Figure 16.4). In addition to its focus on safety, NASCAR (2022) has taken steps to reduce its carbon imprint by switching from leaded fuel to a greener fuel mixture of 15% ethanol and 85% unleaded gasoline.

Students can compare and contrast the carbon footprints of travel methods including walking, bike riding, and driving. As extension activities, they can study how biofuels are produced and identify technologies that make traveling safer—such as safety helmets. They might calculate the travel times for the race cars, RVs, jets, and blimp featured in Blakemore's NASCAR book.

STEAM AMPLIFIERS CHOICE #2—BON APPÉTIT

Some NASCAR fans celebrate their love of racing at tailgate parties. With this in mind, Blakemore included her mother's barbecue sauce and coleslaw recipes in the NASCAR book (Figure 16.5). Blakemore explained how the book's 360° design provided the format for her to pack the book with information, including recipes. Using Blakemore's recipes as inspirations, students will develop a cookbook with illustrations, ingredients,

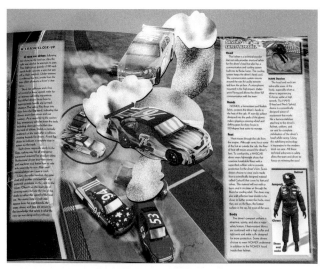

FIGURE 16.4 Sally Blakemore, *NASCAR Pop-Up Book: A Guide to the Sport*, A Crash Close-Up, 2009.
Source: Engineered by Sally Blakemore. Illustrated by Doug Chezem. Photo: Richard Sickler.

FIGURE 16.5 Sally Blakemore, *NASCAR Pop-Up Book: A Guide to the Sport,* Tailgate Party, 2009.
Source: Engineered by Sally Blakemore. Illustrated by Doug Chezem. Photo: Richard Sickler.

and directions focusing on a bon appé-tit (good appetite) theme. Writing reci-pes teaches students procedural writing skills because they must explain step-by-step directions that others can clearly follow. Their recipes will include correct measurement abbreviations. Students can also study STEAM-related food top-ics. For example, students will learn how food is grown through agricultural stud-ies. They might compare and contrast family and industrial farms. They could identify which farming methods are the best for the environment and which ones are harmful. We can collaborate with stu-dents to plant a garden to study growth cycles and learn the skills needed to maintain a healthy garden—i.e. adequate

spacing, healthy soil, weeding, and water-ing. Students might also identify how to store and prepare food safely.

STEAM AMPLIFIERS CHOICE #3—CHAMPIONING DIVERSITY

Working with Blakemore, NASCAR's executives articulated their goal to show the diversity of NASCAR fans. Since the book's publication, NASCAR has taken additional steps to advocate that NASCAR is for all people and is com-mitted to diversity (Figure 16.6). For example, NASCAR (2020) embraced the Black Lives Movement after racer Bubba

FIGURE 16.6 Students can design championing figures as symbols to celebrate humanity's diversity. Sally Blakemore, *NASCAR Pop-Up Book: A Guide to the Sport,* Winning the Race, 2009.
Source: Engineered by Sally Blakemore. Illustrated by Doug Chezem. Photo: Richard Sickler.

Wallace called for the removal of the confederate flag from its events because many people viewed it as a symbol of hate—especially against people of color. NASCAR also makes accommodations for people with disabilities and has written statements of inclusion and support for the LGBTQ+ community. In designing the NASCAR book, Blakemore consciously made sure that book illustrations were respectful of women (personal communication, 2022).

Part of human growth and development is learning how to relate to and empathize with diversified people. Students will learn that **sociology** is a form of science that examines issues and changes in perspectives regarding human rights, gender, class, abilities, and race to form deeper understandings. Using age-appropriate examples, students will identify social issues that impact their schools and communities. For example, they may choose to study how disability is a normal part of the human condition and identify ways to focus on people's abilities. They can study STEAM professionals with disabilities and/or reading barriers, such as Sally Blakemore, and the possible advantages associated with disabilities.

STEAM AMPLIFIERS CHOICE #4—HIP HIP HOORAY: WE CAN TEACH STEAM!

Blakemore's humorous illustrations for Josh Rappaport's *Algebra Survival Guide: A Conversational Handbook for the Thoroughly Befuddled* acknowledge the fears some students may have with mathematics and make learning fun. For example, her *Pitfall* illustration (Figure 16.7) helps students learn algebra through a character that symbolizes how challenging learning can be. Blakemore also takes steps for students to feel victorious with her *Josh and Snake* illustration (Figure 16.8). Given inspirations

FIGURE 16.7 Sally Blakemore's cover illustration *Pitfall* for Josh Rappaport's *Algebra Survival Kit: A Conversational Guide for the Thoroughly Befuddled*, 1998.
Source: © Sally Blakemore.

from Blakemore's book illustrations, students can pick a STEAM subject to create age/ability-level learning manuals for their peers. Students will determine how to create effective illustrations that make learning subject matter fun—even when it feels challenging. They can consider how to enhance their designs with symbols and fonts. Students can work with age/ability-appropriate textbooks, video tutorials, and performance standards to develop their books.

FIGURE 16.8 Sally Blakemore. *Josh and Snake*, updated version, for Josh Rappaport's *Algebra Survival Kit: A Conversational Guide for the Thoroughly Befuddled*, 1998.
Source: © Sally Blakemore.

MOVING FULL STEAM AHEAD...

Sally Blakemore honed her paper engineering skills to design pop-up books that participants enjoy from multiple perspectives. She applied persistence as a young child to work through reading barriers caused by dyslexia and synesthesia and remains persistent in creating innovative designs and working

through publishing regulations, budgets, and deadlines. In relation to her work, we learned about aerodynamic travels, creating recipes, diversity, and teaching STEAM. This chapter concludes Part V of this book. The next chapter describing sites of engagement begins Part VI of this book focusing on the artistic behavior of making creative connections.

References

Blakemore, S. (2017, June 14). More, in fact, is more. *Pacific Standard.* https://psmag.com/education/pop-up-books-more-in-fact-is-more-24240

Cytowic, R., & Eagleman, D. (2011). *Wednesday is indigo blue: Discovering the brain of synesthesia.* The MIT Press.

NASCAR. (2020, June 10). *NASCAR statement on confederate flag.* https://www.nascar.com/news-media/2020/06/10/nascar-statement-on-confederate-flag/

NASCAR. (2022). *NASCAR green: An industry effort.* https://green.nascar.com/nascar-green-an-industry-effort/

Olmon, K. (2009). *In conversation with Sally Blakemore.* Kyle Olmon. http://www.kyleolmon.com/work/articles/blakemore.html

Sickler-Voigt, D. C. (2020). *Teaching and learning in art education: Cultivating students' potential from pre-K through high school.* Routledge.

PART VI

Artists' Lessons to Thrive! Making Creative Connections

Chapter 17

Sites of Engagement

FIGURE 17.1 Marc, Franz (1880–1916). *Yellow Cow (Gelbe Kuh)*. 1911. Oil on canvas. 55 3/8 × 74 1/2 inches (140.5 × 189.2 cm).

Source: Solomon R. Guggenheim Founding Collection. Photo Credit: The Solomon R. Guggenheim Foundation/Art Resource, NY.

Sites of engagement refer to the physical, psychological, cultural, and dialogical spaces people inhabit. They influence our world and provide insights into the ways that people's personal perspectives, relationships, and social dynamics can be influenced by traditions, politics, and economic factors (Blom, 2007; Micheletto-Blouin, 2011). Art often pays homage to the places and spaces that artists have encountered. With this chapter's focus on sites of engagement and artworks by Franz Marc, Mamie Bryan, and Stephan Micheletto-Blouin, we will determine how seemingly different artists share commonalities influenced by their sites of engagement.

FRANZ MARC

Franz Marc was a German Expressionist that belonged to the artist group the Blue Rider known for colorful paintings. His faithful renderings of domestic animals, including *Yellow Cow*, *White Bull*, and *Stables* (Figures 17.1–17.3), come from his close observations of their behaviors

DOI: 10.4324/9781003183693-23

FIGURE 17.2 Marc, Franz (1880–1916). *White Bull (Der Stier)*. 1911. Oil on canvas, 39 3/8 × 53 1/4 inches (100 × 135.2 cm).
Source: Solomon R. Guggenheim Museum, New York. Photo Credit: The Solomon R. Guggenheim Foundation/Art Resource, NY.

in the Bavarian Alps. Marc knew the animals' anatomies and distinct personalities (Carey, 2012). He viewed his Alpine sites of engagement as restful paradises (Schuster, 1988) that became resources for him to construct creative connections between animal subjects, spirituality, and color theory. Portrayed in their natural environments, Marc desired to show the animals' perspectives rather than human ones. He believed that animals had minds and souls. He abstracted their forms and assigned nonnaturalistic colors to represent their spirits. Blue

FIGURE 17.3 Marc, Franz (1880–1916). *Stables*. 1913. Oil on canvas. 29 × 62 inches (73.6 × 157.5 cm).
Source: Solomon R. Guggenheim Founding Collection Photo Credit: The Solomon R. Guggenheim Foundation/Art Resource, NY.

symbolized masculinity, yellow represented femininity, and red referenced the earth (Partsch, 2001). Marc's *Yellow Cow* depicts the cheerful joy of a Fleckvieh cow playfully leaping through a mountainous landscape. Her image dominates the picture plane and exudes her exuberance and harmony with the natural environment, whereas *White Bull* represents the animal's strength of character. Marc emphasized the resting bull's physical mass and serene temperament. The bull's red-colored backside reinforces his deep connections to the earth, while his dreaming state epitomizes peace and harmony.

As World War I approached, Marc's artworks became more abstracted and fragmented. His painting *Stables* represents a stylistic departure from *Yellow Cow* and *White Bull* with its kaleidoscopic design. Its horses' physical forms blend with the surrounding stables and thereby seep their goodness into the environment. Marc equated the purity he saw in animals with war and mistakenly believed that war could cleanse Europe and bring greater good and spiritual awakening (Marc, 2014). While fighting in World War I, Marc ultimately realized that Europe needed better solutions than war. In a letter to his wife, Marc (2014) wrote on New Year 1916: "One must really relearn everything, to rethink it [war], in order to come to terms with this monstrous psychology of fact, ... but [also] to understand the cause and to form counter-thoughts" (pp. 108–109). Just two months after writing this reflection, Marc died in the war. His *Yellow Cow*, *White Bull*, and the horses in *Stables* continue to endure as peaceful symbols to guide humanity and offer better alternatives.

MAMIE BRYAN

Mamie Bryan produced handmade quilts for her family during American racial segregation, World War I, the Great Depression, and World War II. Living on a North Carolina farm, Bryan took care of her family's needs while her husband mined in West Virginia. Farmhouses, like her own, were cold and drafty in winter months due to lack of insulation. Family resources were limited and quilts were necessary for survival. Like other Appalachian women, Bryan made her family's quilts heavy and sturdy and collected materials for their construction (Figure 17.4). Each person needed multiple quilts to stay warm. Because fabric scraps were limited, she salvaged her family's worn-out clothing and collected animal feed sacks made from unbleached muslin—a lightweight, plain-weave cotton fabric. She used the feed sacks for quilt backings (Figure 17.5). Describing her life and quilting, Bryan explained:

> I had to stay here and keep the house and … raise the kids, to get what we've got. It come hard. I had to save everything and piece everything that I could get to make [quilts], to keep us warm…. If I wasn't out in the field working, doing something like that, I was doing something like this [quilting].
> (Bryan & Johnson, 1978)

Bryan needed to produce her quilts quickly due to her many responsibilities. She typically created quilts by piecing together large strips of fabric and used large stitches to save time. *Sixteen Patch Quilt* took Bryan longer to create due to its small pieces.

FIGURE 17.4 Mamie Bryan. *Sixteen Patch Quilt.*
Source: American Folklife Center, Library of Congress.
Photograph BR8-LE31-10 by Lyntha Scott Eiler, 1978.

Bryan's quilts were designed for home use—their natural site of engagement—and would not have been seen in public. Her quilts became known due to the American Folklife Center's Blue Ridge

FIGURE 17.5 Mamie Bryan. *Quilt Back, Feed Sack Logo.*
Source: American Folklife Center, Library of Congress.
Photograph BR8-LE31-16 by Lyntha Scott Eiler, 1978.

FIGURE 17.6 Mamie Bryan showing her quilts to Gerri Johnson.

Source: American Folklife Center, Library of Congress. Photograph BR8-19-20414/16 by Lyntha Scott Eiler, 1978.

Parkway Folklife Project (Figure 17.6) that documented women's traditional quilting practices. Folklorist Gerri Johnson (1981), who met with quilters including Bryan, identified how the Blue Ridge community's quilts represent "the value of home, family, and community" (p. 34). Her research addressed how the quilters' personalities and geographical region shaped the quilts they produced (Johnson, 1981). Bryan applied creative connections to design quilts made with repurposed materials, large stitches, and improvisational designs to keep her family warm. Her quilts correlate with her aesthetic preferences and community influences. The Library of Congress has preserved images of her quilts for all to learn about her place in history.

STEPHAN MICHELETTO-BLOUIN

Stephan Micheletto-Blouin is a contemporary artist who creates artisan-crafted furniture. His sense of design has been influenced by Appalachian craft, The

Krenov School, and renowned woodworkers including James Krenov and Hans Wegner. Excellent craft, functionality, active listening, and how and where his works will be used are essential qualities that form the creative connections that Micheletto-Blouin applies to produce furniture (Figures 17.7–17.9). For example, Micheletto-Blouin designed *Weaving Bench* (Figure 17.7) to accommodate his wife Amanda's creative needs as a textile artist working on a loom. His weaving bench includes a seat height perfectly suited to Amanda's body and proportions that work in harmony with her loom's dimensions. Adding to the bench's comfort and practicality, Micheletto-Blouin designed sliding drawers to store weaving supplies.

In addition to listening to people's design needs, Micheletto-Blouin's process of active listening involves the wood he selects. He applies his cognitive awareness of design, manual skills, purposeful intent, and intuition to discover what each form can become. He matches pieces of lumber and works with each piece's natural grainlines, knots, and burls.

FIGURE 17.7 Stephan Micheletto-Blouin. *Weaving Bench in Canary and Sycamore.* 2018.
Source: ©Stephan Micheletto-Blouin.

FIGURE 17.8 Stephan Micheletto-Blouin. *Commodities Bench*. 2013. Ash slab, pallet, banding, soil, grass.
Source: © Stephan Micheletto-Blouin.

Whereas *Weaving Bench* centers on functionality and design, Micheletto-Blouin's *Commodities Bench* (Figure 17.8) takes discourse to the forefront by bringing awareness to the raw materials and resources needed to produce woodcrafts. Issues including mass production, the usurp of natural resources, polluting plastics, and global industrial practices are not to be missed. After exhibiting *Commodities Bench* as a thought piece, Micheletto-Blouin repurposed its wood into a slide for his sons, thereby forming an entirely new site of engagement for enjoyment and play within the home (Figure 17.9).

FIGURE 17.9 Stephan Micheletto-Blouin's son Rex demonstrates how he uses his slide. *Commodities Bench Slide*.
Source: © Stephan Micheletto-Blouin.

Describing his works, Micheletto-Blouin explained, "these are human in scale and presentation. The fact that you could lift, hold, or hug these objects is important to how we come to them" (personal communication, 2021). He wants people to notice his furnishings' fine details and invites people to "discover that the back of a drawer is dovetailed beautifully, the bottom of the table is finished, [and] the top or the back frame of a cabinet is designed with as much care as the door" (personal communication, 2021). These features are rarely seen in mass-produced furniture. His overall goal is for people to experience his works as sites of engagement that are well-designed, friendly, and relatable. Interacting with each of Micheletto-Blouin's artworks, people can spark conversations about what they see, feel, and experience and address the complex issues that resolve around craft and material production.

BUILDING CREATIVE CONNECTIONS

Studying Marc's, Bryan's, and Micheletto-Blouin's art, students can learn how sites of engagement can connect seemingly different artworks. The artists' personalized creative connections broaden our understandings of the places, spaces, and meanings that inspire artistic productions. Marc learned the forms, characteristics, and personalities of the animals he painted. He demonstrated empathy for the animals and viewed them as spiritual inspirations. Bryan learned how to work with limited materials in her rural community to produce functional quilts. She safeguarded her family by providing for their care, comfort, and well-being. Micheletto-Blouin's knowledge of wood enables him to manipulate its various forms and produce high-quality furniture. His art brings awareness to design in family life and the need to protect the earth's natural resources.

Teaching and Learning in the STEAM Artist's Studio 17.1 examines how sites of

---

Teaching and Learning in the STEAM Artist's Studio 17.1

Introduce students to Marc's, Bryan's, and Micheletto-Blouin's art and the meaning of sites of engagement that include physical locations, virtual spaces, and personal mindsets. Then, have students identify how each artist utilized creative connections to produce their art and compare and contrast how their artworks share similarities and differences. Next, ask students to describe places that have personal significance to them and how they can create art influenced by these spaces.

Essential/Guiding Questions

1. How have sites of engagement influenced Marc's, Bryan's, and Micheletto-Blouin's art?
2. Describe the artists' abilities to form creative connections. Why are they significant?

Daily Learning Targets

As an artist, I can identify a site of engagement that is relevant to me and design an artwork inspired by its meaning.

- I can select the art media of my choice and make revisions to find the best visual solutions to create my design.
- I can create a unified artwork that demonstrates craftspersonship.
- I can explain how the artwork I produced was informed by the creative connections I made to communicate meanings about my chosen site of engagement.

National Core Arts Anchor Standards NVAS 3, 5, 8, and 10.
www.nationalartsstandards.org

Teaching for Students' Development

PK-12: (A) Explain how STEAM professionals pull from different ideas and make connections to develop creative solutions. (B) Ask students to consider how Marc's, Bryan's, and Micheletto-Blouin's choices of subject matter and/or materials were influenced by their sites of engagement.

Early childhood: Young students understand sites of engagement through concrete examples. Focus instruction on physical places and their people, objects, and materials when describing sites of engagement.

Middle childhood: Students combine concrete thinking skills with logical reasoning skills to understand relationships and see alternative possibilities. Have students look to evidence in Marc's, Bryan's, and Micheletto-Blouin's artworks and ask "what if" questions to identify how possible changes might alter the meanings of their artworks.

Early adolescence: Middle school students are transitioning from concrete learning skills to understanding abstract concepts. Ask students to consider how virtual reality produces new sites of engagement. Then have them compare and contrast examples of virtual sites of engagement with physical ones.

Adolescence: High school students understand abstract concepts more clearly. Ask students to identify how the global community is shaped by global perceptions and humanity's interconnectedness. Have students brainstorm ways that sites of engagement can be experienced on a global level.

engagements inspired Marc's, Bryan's, and Micheletto-Blouin's creative artmaking approaches. Its *STEAM Amplifiers* teach about healthy living and biological life-cycle assessment.

STEAM AMPLIFIERS CHOICE #1—CELEBRATING HEALTHY LIVING

Healthy living aligns with Marc's, Bryan's, and Micheletto-Blouin's sites of engagement. Viewing Marc's *White Bull* and *Stables*, students can discuss how their bodies feel when they have enough sleep and rest compared to when they do not. Each day, children up to age 5 need between 10–13 hours of sleep; children ages 6–13 need 9–11 hours of sleep; and adolescents 14 and over need 8–10 hours of sleep (Centers for Disease Control and Prevention (CDC), 2022). Reflecting on these statistics, students can identify the things that facilitate sleep, such as a quiet,

dark room. They may enjoy comfortable quilts—like the ones Mamie Bryan created, cozy pillows, and/or stuffed animals. Students can discuss what makes sleep more difficult, such as bright screens, loud noises, text notifications, caffeine, and stress.

Movement, like sleep, is important for the body's health. Referencing the leaping motion of Franz Marc's *Yellow Cow* and Stephan Micheletto-Blouin's slide, students can talk about the different ways that they move their bodies through play and exercise. The CDC (2022) recommends that children ages 3–5 move continuously throughout the day and those 6 and older participate in at least 60 minutes "of moderate-to-vigorous intensity physical activity each day." Their Healthy Schools website offers resources for teachers, parents, and students and also includes National Health Education Standards with strategies for integrating health education into the school curriculum. Children benefit by participating in exercises that include aerobic activities, strength-building exercises, bone-building exercises, and stretches. In addition to discussions about healthy sleep and exercise habits, students can collaborate with teachers to identify ways to integrate movement into the school day. They can also create a healthy living journal that includes written reflections, sketches, and mathematical charts about sleep and exercise.

STEAM AMPLIFIERS CHOICE #2—BIOLOGICAL LIFECYCLE ASSESSMENT

The animals illustrated in Marc's paintings, the muslin feed sacks that formed Bryan's *Sixteen Patch Quilt*, and the wood in Micheletto-Blouin's furniture progressed through lifecycles. A **biological lifecycle** describes the series of stages of all living organisms from the inception of life through death. Students can study the lifecycles of Marc's animals, including his favorite animal the horse (Figure 17.10). When discussing the horse's lifecycle, students can identify the horse's physical changes and the best ways to care for horses at the different stages of their life.

Examining Appalachian quilts made from repurposed muslin feed sacks by people of diverse ethnic and socioeconomic backgrounds during the first half of the 20th century, including the Great Depression, students can study the lifecycle of cotton and its progression from seeds, seedlings, to its blossoms, cotton bolls, and dried cotton balls. As part of their studies, students can learn that engineers make **lifecycle assessments** of the products we use to determine their efficiency. They identify the extents that products are built to last, conserve energy, and use renewable/nonrenewable resources in production. For example, 99% of the cotton used in today's industry is nonorganic (Chang, 2017). Nonorganic cotton has a heavy carbon footprint—requiring substantial water and harmful pesticides and insecticides to grow. By repurposing cotton fabric scraps into other useful products like Appalachian quilt makers did and growing organic cotton, today's society can minimize waste resulting from nonorganic cotton production. Delving into cotton's history, students can learn about the cotton gin and how its 1793 invention greatly expanded cotton production. It fueled injustices including the Indian Removal Act of 1830 and increased the domestic slave trade. Learning for Justice's *K-12 Framework for Teaching American Slavery* is a helpful resource for teaching students how "Slavery and the slave trade were central to the development and growth of the colonial economies and what is now the United States" (Southern Poverty Law Center, 2018–2022, p. 3) and how cotton textile manufacturing enriched international businesses.

Using Micheletto-Blouin's art as inspiration, students can study the lifecycle of trees. They can illustrate how they grow from germinating seeds, sprout, become saplings, and grow into full-sized trees. Students can examine how a research team made lifecycle assessments of chairs and identified that wooden chairs last longer and produce a smaller carbon footprint than ones made from plastic and aluminum (Wu et al., 2019). The types of wood used and the strength of joints also impact a chair's lifecycle assessment. In their assessment, the research team found that only 56% of the wood needed for the chair's production became part of the chair. The remaining 44% resulted in waste material. In addition to these facts, students can study how chairs' development requires gas and electricity for product transportation.

Horse Lifecycle

- **Foal**: 0 to under 12 months old. A foal who has weaned is called a **weanling**.
- **Yearling**: 1–2 years old.
- **Adolescent**: 2–3 years old. Males are called **colts** and females **fillies**.
- **Adulthood**: 4 years old and older. Males are called **stallions** and females **mares**.
- **Elderly**: Late teens to 20 years old.

MOVING FULL STEAM AHEAD...

This chapter described how Marc, Bryan, and Micheletto-Blouin developed artworks that connected to their sites of engagement and were informed by their interests, needs, and available resources. In correlation to their art, we learned about

FIGURE 17.10 Franz Marc, *Birth of the Horses*, 1913, Color Woodcut on Japanese Paper, 35.5 cm × 25.4 cm (14" × 10").
Source: Städtische Galerie im Lenbachhaus und Kunstbau München. (CC0 1.0).

healthy living and biological lifecycle assessment. The next chapter continues with the artistic behavior of making creative connections describing how complied data can inform art and design.

References

Blom, I. (2007). *On the style site: Art, sociality, and media culture*. Sternberg.

Bryan, M., & Johnson, G. N. (1978, September 10). *"I never had time for fooling."* [Interview]. American Folklife Center, Library of Congress. https://www.loc.gov/item/qlt000007/

Carey, J. (2012). *Franz Marc as an ethologist*. [Master's thesis, University of South Florida]. https://digitalcommons.usf.edu/etd/4005

Centers for Disease Control and Prevention. (2022). *CDC healthy schools*. https://www.cdc.gov/healthyschools/index.htm

Chang, A. [TedEd]. (2017). *The lifecycle of a t-shirt*. [Video]. YouTube. https://www.youtube.com/watch?v=BiSYoeqb_VY

Johnson, G. N. (1981). *Blue Ridge quilts—Plain and fancy*. American Folklife Center, Library of Congress. https://www.loc.gov/item/afc1982009_11_134/

Marc, F. (2014). *Briefe aus dem feld. 1914–1916* [ebook edition]. Allitera Verlag.

Micheletto-Blouin, S. (2011). *Toward relational craft.* [Master's thesis, East Carolina University]. https://thescholarship.ecu.edu/handle/10342/3758

Partsch, S. (2001). *Franz Marc.* Taschen.

Schuster, P. (1988). *Franz Marc: Postcards to Prince Jussuf.* Prestel.

Southern Poverty Law Center. (2018–2022). A quick reference guide to teaching hard history: A K-12 framework for teaching American slavery. https://www.learningforjustice.org/sites/default/files/2022-12/LFJ-Quick-Reference-Guide-Teaching-Hard-History-K-12-Framework-December-2022-12092022.pdf

Wu, F., Haviarova, E., & Helfrich, J. (2019). *Life-cycle inventory of hardwood lumber school chair.* Purdue University. https://www.purdue.edu/woodresearch/wp-content/uploads/2019/12/LCA_1-KH.pdf

Chapter 18

Art, Design, and Compiled Data

FIGURE 18.1 Antoni Gaudi, *Sagrada Familia*. Exterior at night.
Source: Euku, (CC BY-SA 3.0), Wikimedia Commons.

Reliable data sources shape society's knowledge about STEAM creators' products, artworks, and designs. Scholars compile data from **primary sources** that include original artworks, letters, diagrams, models, and statements, as well as **secondary sources** that include reproductions and all other sources. This chapter examines how compiled data and technologies have broadened society's understandings of built environment sites of engagement including Antoni Gaudi's *Sagrada Familia*, the Met Museum's *Architectural Model of the Temple of King Solomon* and *Damascus Room*, and Violet Oakley's *Pennsylvania State Capitol building murals*.

ANTONI GAUDI

Antoni Gaudi developed iconic architectural structures in the Moderniste style featuring organic forms, fluid lines,

DOI: 10.4324/9781003183693-24

vibrant colors, and exciting textures augmented by integrated mosaics, stained glass, and wrought iron. Gaudi's *Sagrada Familia* (Figures 18.1 and 18.2), a basilica located in Barcelona, is one of seven of Gaudi's architectural structures identified on UNESCO's World Heritage List. Its name means holy family.

Shortly after *Sagrada Familia's* first cornerstone was laid in 1882, its original architect Francisco de Paula del Villar resigned due to disagreements with Josep Marià Bocabella, who commissioned his work. Gaudi began working as lead architect in 1884 and understood construction would take more than a lifetime to complete. Building on Villar's neogothic designs, Gaudi spent 43 years developing elaborate plans and models to guide those who would follow him. Only *Sagrada Familia's* crypt, apse, and part of the Nativity façade were completed at the time of Gaudi's death in 1926. Ten years later—during the Spanish Civil War, anarchists ransacked Gaudi's workshop. Architect Francesc de Paula Quintana spent years reconstructing Gaudi's fragmented models so that *Sagrada Familia's* construction could resume in the 1950s.

Subsequent teams of architects, engineers, and artists have carried on Gaudi's work. Since 2012, Jordi Faulí has served as *Sagrada Familia's* head architect. He exclaimed, "Gaudí left us the path…. Sometimes, though, we've had to work hard to find it" (Abend, 2019). Surviving primary and secondary sources have allowed *Sagrada Familia's* design team to understand and engineer Gaudi's plans. The design team has utilized lidar scanning (see Chapter 4) to produce accurate 3D models, 3D printers, and computer numerical control (CNC) milling machines for stone cutting. Senior architect Mark Burry conceived the idea of using three-dimensional aeronautical drafting software to deconstruct Gaudi's most challenging designs, including the complex hyperboloid and paraboloid forms within the basilica's interior. Its massive columns look like trees with elegant hyperboloid vaults replicating the feel of a protective canopy (Figures 18.2 and 18.3). These tree-like columns provide a humbling sensation to connect those in their presence to God. Stained-glass windows enhance this sensation with their kaleidoscopic palette of illuminating light.

By applying new technologies to Gaudi's models, the design team has

FIGURE 18.2 *Sagrada Familia's* nave interior contains multicolored stone columns, decorative capitals, hyperboloid vaults, and stained glass.
Source: Sagrada Família (oficial), (CC BY-SA 3.0), Wikimedia Commons.

FIGURE 18.3 *Sagrada Familia's* columns and vaulting resemble a forest.
Source: SBA73 from Sabadell, Catalunya, (CC BY-SA 2.0), Wikimedia Commons.

solved complex problems in a "living laboratory for experimentation" (Burry in CIMNE MC, 2019) and can work faster. When completed, *Sagrada Familia* will be the tallest church measuring 566 feet (172.5 meters) consisting of three façades (nativity, passion, and glory) and 18 spires representing the 12 Apostles, 4 Evangelists, the Virgin Mary, and Jesus.

ARCHITECTURAL MODEL OF THE TEMPLE OF KING SOLOMON

In 1887, *Architectural Model of the Temple of King Solomon* (Figure 18.4) was exhibited at the *Anglo-Jewish Historical Exhibition* along with numerous artworks, cultural artifacts, models, and informative documents designed to teach the public about Jewish history, culture, art (Judaica), and Jewish people in England (Berger, 2018). The organizers aimed to use its teachings to develop positive relations between Anglo and Jewish communities, alert

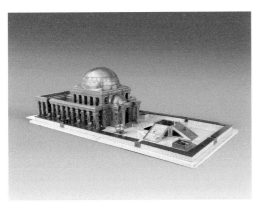

FIGURE 18.4 *Architectural Model of the Temple of King Solomon in Jerusalem*, 1883, after a design by Thomas Newberry. Carved and gilded by Messrs. Bartlet. Gilded silver and brass appurtenances by W. Spurrier. Length: 7′ 8″ (234 cm); Width: 3′ 8″ (112 cm).

Source: www.metmuseum.org. (CC0 1.0)

society about the harms that resulted from anti-Semitic propaganda, and secure equal rights for Jews.

The *Architectural Model* was constructed after Thomas Newberry's designs. Newberry, a biblical scholar, made careful English translations of the Hebrew Bible's descriptions of King Solomon's Temple—Jerusalem's first temple (957 BCE). His translations provided exact information about the temple's architectural layout and assembly at Mount Moriah. The temple included side chambers, galleries, a porch, the holy place, and the Holy of Holies—the temple's most sacred room that housed the ark, a cabinet that contains the two stone tablets written with the ten commandments. Newberry's (n.d.) translations described how the temple's builders preserved the temple's tranquility by operating loud construction equipment off-site: "The building will be noiselessly erected, and no sound heard but the sound of triumph and of praise when the top stone is added to the whole" (p. 24). Due to Solomon's extensive wealth, the temple was built using the finest materials, and only the highest priests were allowed to enter.

Newberry (n.d.) translated the descriptions of the temple's ornate features. "The floor was covered with gold. On the walls and ceiling were carved work of cedar covered with solid gold, fitted upon the carved work, glittering with precious stones" (p. 18). Interior possessions included ten gold tables and seventy lamps. Decorative carvings symbolized God's divine connections to humanity. Newberry (n.d.) explained his inclusion of the temple's dome: "The marginal reading for beams is 'vaulted beams,' which implies the vaulted ceiling of the holy place, and the dome surmounting the whole" (p. 20). This exceptional feature made his model distinctive because the dome was not directly identified in the Bible (The Metropolitan Museum of Art, 2000–2022).

DAMASCUS ROOM

Damascus Room is a **qa'a**, a winter reception chamber dating to the late Ottoman period (Figure 18.5). Dismantled from its original Syrian location, *Damascus Room* was part of a private home belonging to affluent owners from 1707–1930s CE. It faced the north side of the home's courtyard, which offered greater warmth in the winter. Entering the qa'a antechamber, called the **ataba**, guests observed a fountain and a **masab**, a decorative niche commonly displayed in Islamic architecture. Colorful light from stained glass windows permeated the room and reflected on its **ajami,** decorative relief wood panels covered with painted metallic tin and gold leaf. Only special guests were invited into the qa'a's upper level called a **tazar**, where they sat on raised cushioned seating, tasted epicurean foods and beverages, and admired the room's ornate features.

FIGURE 18.5 This *Damascus Room* detail shows its masab. 1707.

Source: www.metmuseum.org. (CC0 1.0)

Damascus Room's ceiling cornice, wall cornice, and wall panels feature poetry written in calligraphy that establishes the owner's Muslim faith and describes the room's spring décor (Kenney, 2011). Calligraphy is venerated in Islamic art for its aesthetic and spiritual values. Although the room's poetry identifies the owner as a descendant of the Prophet Mohamed, *Damascus Room's* provenance remains unknown because the owner's name and its original location were not recorded. Writing on a 1930s photograph of the qa'a indicates that it came from Damascus's southwest region. In 2010–12 when *Damascus Room* was relocated from its original 1970 installation, the Met Museum's conservation team discovered original installation errors. A numbering system on the back of its wooden panels identifying the panels' correct order had not been followed. The panels' correct arrangements in the reinstallation brought clarity to the poems' meanings. As two-wall panels are housed in a different collection, the team printed high-resolution photograph reproductions to illustrate their missing content.

For enhanced accuracy, the conservation team sought external verity and studied Ottoman interiors. They learned that *Damascus Room's* floor tiles had originally belonged to its courtyard. Its fountain, built at an earlier date, had also been moved from its original location. Photographs from the 1930s revealed missing flat cornice boards that framed the room.

The team performed ultraviolet radiation illumination to examine the ajamis' pigments. Multiple coats of varnish applied over the years dramatically darkened the room's calligraphy and paintings. The team's study revealed that the varnish dissolved the original pigment. Therefore, they decided to keep the varnish intact to conserve the original work.

VIOLET OAKLEY'S PENNSYLVANIA CAPITOL MURALS

Best known for her creation of 43 murals at the Pennsylvania State Capitol building (Figure 18.6), Violet Oakley established a prolific career when women rarely earned public art commissions. Oakley was contracted by architect Joseph Huston in 1902 to create the capitol building's Governor's Reception Room murals titled *The Founding of the State of Liberty Spiritual* because he believed that a woman's artistic perspective would "act as an encouragement of the women of the state" (Ricci, 2019). These murals illustrate the historic events that shaped the Reformation and influenced William Penn, the founder of the English Colony Commonwealth of Pennsylvania. Oakley was deeply inspired by Penn, a Quaker, who advocated for religious freedom and pacifist principles of goodwill and peace.

Given the lead capitol artist's sudden death, Oakley was also commissioned to design the Senate Chamber murals with designs that teach about *The Creation and Preservation of the Union* and Supreme Court Chamber murals. Oakley's Senate Chamber murals contain portraits of Abraham Lincoln and George Washington. Additional murals reinforce Penn's pacifist philosophy. For example, she depicted Quakers' opposition to slavery by illustrating how they paid a ship captain to transport the enslaved peoples on his ship to freedom in Nova Scotia.

Oakley' Senate Chamber's centerpiece mural, *International Understanding and Unity*, contains a wise, colossal-sized heroine in a blue robe (Figure 18.7). She personifies the water of life—a unifying force. Her outstretched arms give the impression of embracing the Senate Chamber with its fine American Renaissance architectural features and décor. Surrounding the water of life heroine, Oakley painted a city of peace where wars end and military leaders lay down their weapons, and slavery is abolished.

Oakley spent 25 years producing the Pennsylvania State Capitol murals. Her mural designs resulted from her extensive readings, notes, and illustrations on their subject matter. She traveled to Italy to examine Renaissance frescoes and Oxford

FIGURE 18.6 Violet Oakley's murals enhance Pennsylvania State Capitol's Senate Chamber.
Source: Photo: © Amy Sparwasser, Flickr.

FIGURE 18.7 Violet Oakley. *International Understanding and Unity*, detail.
Source: Photo: © Amy Sparwasser, Flickr.

to study the history of law. When hearing that the history of law had never been written, Oakley responded "then I'll have to write it" (Woodmere Art Museum, 2019). She brought to life her interpretation of the law's history in Pennsylvania's Supreme Court Chamber. Its *Devine Law* mural features the illuminated letters L. A. W. that symbolized to Oakley "love and wisdom." Oakley's capitol murals teach moral and civic lessons. Throughout her lifetime, she advocated for equity for all people, social justice, religious freedom, and international peace. She wanted others to understand her murals' messages that present pathways to goodness with love as the triumphing force. She regularly visited the capitol to teach lawmakers and the public about their meanings. After Oakley's passing in 1961, her life partner Edith Emerson perpetuated Oakley's legacy by preserving and exhibiting her documents, art, and photographs for society's benefit.

BUILDING CREATIVE CONNECTIONS

Studying Antoni Gaudi's *Sagrada Familia, Damascus Room, Architectural Model of the Temple of King Solomon in Jerusalem,* and Violet Oakley's Pennsylvania Senate Chamber murals demonstrate the value of compiling data to develop and preserve built environment sites of engagement. Rich and accurate data are essential to STEAM studies. They build creative connections that assist society in understanding artists' intents, (re)constructing artists' designs, and conserving historical works. *Teaching and Learning in the STEAM Artist's Studio 18.1* builds on the artistic behavior of making creative connections through students' development of portfolios centering on sites of engagement. Its *STEAM Amplifiers* teach about inclusive and accessible public places through 3D printing and creating with augmented realities.

Teaching and Learning in the STEAM Artist's Studio 18.1

Invite students to compare and contrast this chapter's sites of engagement. Have them identify how primary and secondary data sources aid society in understanding the built environment and its inspired designs. Ask students to brainstorm how built environment spaces result from artists' and designers' creative connections that teach society about people's needs, values, and beliefs.

Essential/Guiding Questions

1. How do this chapter's sites of engagement (a basilica, temple, home, and senate chamber) and the data associated with their development and preservation influence our understandings of them?
2. How did Gaudi and Oakley take steps to preserve the meanings of their work? Why was it important to them? Why do museums and other public

spaces display, preserve, and teach about art—including the *Architectural Model of the Temple of King Solomon* and *Damascus Room* in the Met Museum's collection?

Daily Learning Targets

As an artist/designer, I can design a project portfolio about a built environment site of engagement that I have designed.

- I can identify who will use the site and make creative connections to develop designs that suit its purpose.
- I can integrate quality forms of documentation as data to demonstrate my project's development, goals, and outcomes.
- I can present my completed project portfolio and include resources (i.e., artist statement, interview, written report) to teach others about my work.

National Core Arts Anchor Standards NVAS 3, 5, 9, and 11. www.nationalartsstandards.org

Teaching for Students' Development

PK-12: (A) Explain to students the value of making plans, asking questions, and creating models to problem solve and make creative connections before producing final designs like artists and designers do. (B) Present religious subject matter as means for understanding creative works in context and the diversity of people's beliefs without demonstrating a preference for one religion or political perspective over another.

Early childhood: Young children benefit from practicing new skills, including how to collect and store materials in a portfolio. Guide students in portfolio development and review procedures so that they become familiar to students.

Middle childhood: Students enjoy explaining how they learn new skills and can share their strategies for collecting data and creating designs. Reinforce strategies to include necessary details and academic vocabulary in their descriptions and portfolio presentations to peers.

Early adolescence: Middle school students are developing deductive reasoning skills. Use probing questions to guide students in learning how to apply them as they study sites of engagement and present their portfolios.

Adolescence: High school students utilize deductive reasoning skills to solve problems. Invite students to identify problems in existing built environment spaces of their choosing and explain how design changes could improve their usability, quality, and/or accessibility. Have students demonstrate how they designed works in their portfolios to solve problems.

STEAM AMPLIFIERS CHOICE #1—INCLUSIVE 3D PRINTING

Built environment spaces connect to the themes of inclusion, accessibility, and belonging. Incorporating this chapter's examples, students can discuss the importance of designing inclusive and accessible spaces where everyone can participate and identify when barriers exist. *Sagrada Familia* has an entrance fee but is free on certain days. Only priests could enter King Solomon's Temple. Intergenerational family members were permitted to use *Damascus Room* when honored male guests were not present. Violet Oakley broke gender barriers by receiving unprecedented public commissions for her work in the Pennsylvania State Capitol Building. Her achievements hold significant value in LGBTQ+ history.

Students can design inclusive and accessible models using **3D printing**, an additive manufacturing printing process. There are many free and affordable Computer-Aided Design (CAD) software applications for students to create 3D designs including, Morphi, and SketchUp. STL (stereolithography) files convert or slice digital designs into individual layers, which serve as instructions for the 3D printer to create the prints. Most classrooms and school makerspaces use a Fused Deposition Modeling (FDM) 3D printer that extracts thermoplastic from a nozzle that builds up thin layers to print the desired 3D form. If a 3D printer is unavailable, students can still use the CAD software to model three-dimensional forms as a guide for constructing sculptures by hand.

Students can research real-world examples of 3D printing's applications—such as constructing *Sagrada Familia*. Students

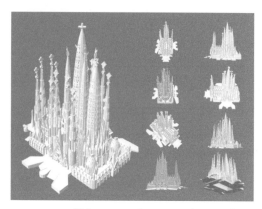

FIGURE 18.8 This screen-shot compilation of an STL file illustrates 3D views of *Sagrada Familia*. *Source: Revtec3D, Thingiverse (CC BY 4.0).*

can access open-source 3D models of *Sagrada Familia* (Figure 18.8) and other structures to foster greater understandings of their forms and watch online videos of artists' and designers' use of applications for 3D printing.

STEAM AMPLIFIERS CHOICE #2—AUGMENTED REALITIES

Augmented reality (AR) is an interactive experience that superimposes digital content upon a real-world environment, such as an interior (Figure 18.9) or outdoor

FIGURE 18.9 Flash augmented reality using Papervision 3D. *Source: Thomas Geersing, Flickr, (CC by 2.0).*

space. It differs from **virtual reality**, which is a total emersion experience in a digital world. Students can apply TinkerCAD, Morphi, SketchUp, and other apps they use for 3D printing to produce AR experiences in real time. Using a viewing technology, such as a tablet, AR assists students in understanding concepts from multiple perspectives and forming visualizations. Students can also experiment with other AR apps used by professionals. For example, contractors use magicplan, an AR and lidar Scanning app, to measure the layout of a room, make estimates, and design floorplans. Using the camera on a handheld device, the app can scan a room's square footage and ceiling height. The app provides students with inspirations to study math skills including area, surface, volume, ratios, and scale as they create built environment designs. For supplemental studies, students can examine the many ways that STEAM professionals, including artists, architects, and museum educators, are using AR.

MOVING FULL STEAM AHEAD...

This chapter furthered our studies on the artistic behavior of making creative connections with examinations of Antoni Gaudi's *Sagrada Familia*; *Damascus Room*; *Architectural Model of the Temple of King Solomon in Jerusalem*; and Violet Oakley's Pennsylvania Senate Chamber murals. It described how compiled data shape our understandings of STEAM and sites of engagement. We made connections to 3D printing and AR. In the next chapter, we will apply the theme going places to continue our studies on making creative connections.

References

Abend, L. (2019). Gaudi's great temple. *TIME Magazine, 194*(2), 30–39.

Berger, N. (2018). *The Jewish museum: History and memory, identity and art from Vienna to the Bezalel National Museum, Jerusalem.* Brill.

CIMNE MC. (2019, December 11). *Antoni Gaudi architect and structural artist—M. Burry.* [Video]. YouTube. https://www.youtube.com/watch?v=oiofvf_4EcY

Kenney, E. (2011). *Heilbrunn timeline of art history: The Damascus Room.* The Metropolitan Museum of Art. https://www.metmuseum.org/toah/hd/dama/hd_dama.htm

Newberry, T. (n.d.). *The temples of Solomon and Ezekiel* (2nd edition). Pickering & Inglis. https://www.brethrenarchive.org/media/363598/newbery-t-_-the-temples-of-solomon-and-ezekiel.pdf

Ricci, P. L. (2019, Fall). To form a more perfect union: Violet Oakley's murals in the Pennsylvania Senate Chamber. *Pennsylvania Heritage.* https://paheritage.wpengine.com/article/form-perfect-union-violet-oakley-murals-pennsylvania-senate-chamber/

The Metropolitan Museum of Art. (2000–2022). *Architectural model of the temple of King Solomon in Jerusalem.* https://www.metmuseum.org/art/collection/search/786829?searchField=All&sortBy=Relevance&showOnly=openAccess&ft=jewish&offset=80&rpp=80&pos=98

Woodmere Art Museum [WoodmereArtMuseum]. (2019, April 8). *Violet Oakley—Capitol all three chambers.* [Video]. YouTube. https://www.youtube.com/watch?v=B-Mq61w8Ycs

Chapter 19

Let's Go Places!

FIGURE 19.1 Betye Saar, *Wishing for Winter*, 1989. Mixed media. 40 3/4 × 19 1/4 × 2 1/4 in. (103.6 × 48.9 × 5.8 cm.).

Source: Smithsonian American Art Museum. © Betye Saar.

DOI: 10.4324/9781003183693-25

Going places exudes excitement. It refers to the physical act of changing locations, traveling, and seeing new sites, as well as signifies bringing ideas, dreams, and aspirations to fruition, eliminating barriers, moving up in the world, and making positive marks on society. The themes of going places and sites of engagement unite artists Betye Saar, Patti Warashina, and Susan Brandeis given their artistic representations of motion, times, and places. Going places also exemplifies these artists' accomplishments and the sophisticated meanings that drive their work. Specializing in different media, Saar, Warashina, and Brandeis generated comprehensive understandings of their media's unique qualities and used them to make creative connections that teach important societal lessons.

BETYE SAAR

Betye Saar transforms recycled materials into **assemblages**—artworks that she constructs by arranging objects onto a background surface to produce aesthetic designs. She repurposes vintage keepsakes including gloves, clocks, and other memorabilia, which provide inspirations for Saar to articulate stories about life, family, and the African-American community (MoAD, 2018). Saar's designs form creative connections that link the past and present. Her assemblage *Wishing for Winter* feels reminiscent of dressing up to visit a café and enjoy warm beverages and intimate conversations (Figure 19.1). Its window frame gives the impression of looking in and experiencing a friendly gathering. A faded photograph and a fragmented book indicate sentimental memories. An elegant black glove takes center stage. Similar to the prehistoric stamped human hands that personified cave walls and represented people's livelihoods, Saar's glove marks its wearer's established place in the world. Scattered butterfly wings and a bird's wing nestled in the lower right corner feel like dynamic forces that transport the glove's wearer to where she wants to go—a cooler time of year. The wings represent beauty and elegance, just like the lady's glove. Keys can be interpreted as symbolic tools that unlock the present moment and make Saar's wish for winter come true.

Saar balances sentimental works like *Wishing for Winter* with critically acclaimed artworks that confront racism. For example, her assemblage *Liberation of Aunt Jemima* (1972) advocates for equality and change with its central mammy figure, a heavily branded caricature of a smiling caregiver designed to perpetuate the erroneous belief that black women who were enslaved lived happily in domestic servitude. Whereas *Wishing for Winter's* wings and keys operate as symbols for blissful change, Saar designed her Aunt Jemima as a warrior with guns that she carries as symbols of force, rather than violence, to empower the mammy, transport her out of servitude, and correct misrepresentations of her identity. Describing Aunt Jemima, Saar expressed, "As an artist, I feel that I'm a warrior too, in my own way of taking discards, of taking things that are thrown away, [and] putting them together, which may or may not change the way people think about them" (MoAD, 2018). Nearly half a century after Saar's creation of the *Liberation of Aunt Jemima*, the Aunt Jemima caricature that branded pancake mix and syrup for 131 years received her wings of freedom and keys to equity given the public's continued demands for change that prompted the company to rename its products and remove the mammy logo from its packaging. These positive outcomes demonstrate the power of Saar's artistic messaging and her ability to change people's perceptions.

PATTI WARASHINA

Patti Warashina's *Convertible Car Kiln* signifies going places and radiates creative fun. Warashina's representational hybrid hotrod design invites audiences to reinvestigate their understandings of cars and kilns (Figure 19.2). Her symbolic fusion produces creative connections that transformed a convertible automobile into something new—a car capable of firing ceramic pieces. Gold and silver strands radiate from the hotrod's core and symbolize the glowing flames needed to fire clay. The flames also reinforce the sizzling excitement of the hotrod's sleek design and fast speed. When Warashina started creating in clay, artists generally preferred a loose,

FIGURE 19.2 Patti Warashina, *Convertible Car Kiln*, 1971. Earthenware, gold and silver luster glaze, and Plexiglas, 14 1/2 × 35 1/2 × 14 1/2 in. (36.9 × 90.2 × 36.9 cm).

Source: Smithsonian American Art Museum. © Patti Warashina.

non-representational abstract expressionist style. Warashina differed by producing realistic, tighter-formed ceramic sculptures. Inspired by Surrealism, Warashina reinterpreted recognizable objects to make them feel familiar and also shockingly different.

Over her career, Warashina has developed a solid command of clay. She understands its unique qualities and has the technical proficiencies to construct the forms she desires. Despite her exceptional skills, Warashina admits that clay takes a lifetime to learn because of its challenging variables: "In ceramics you can put the mark down, hope it stays that way, and when you put it in the magic box [kiln], it either cracks or it changes colors, or it runs" (Jeck, 2005).

Convertible Car Kiln is Warashina's response to needing to gain technical proficiencies with clay, glazes, and kilns. She learned to calculate the appropriate British thermal units (BTUs) for firing determined by the needed end kiln temperature, kiln volume and material, and time necessary to reach the desired end temperature in the kiln. Women had been purposely excluded from these important learning opportunities. Warashina explained:

> When I was in school, the conversations about kiln construction and BTUs were aimed at men. It was assumed that women were china painters and would get married, stay at home, and have babies, while the clay world belonged to the men … In response to this macho attitude, I started making my own kilns!
>
> (Smithsonian American Art Museum, n.d., para. 3)

Combining clever design and wit, Warashina tackled misperceptions about females being able to understand masculine-dominated kiln and hotrod cultures by gaining technical strengths in clay and constructing the hotrod with the kiln as an efficient hybrid-ceramic form. *Convertible Car Kiln* also demonstrates Warashina's ability to navigate and participate in these worlds, thereby reinforcing women's abilities to move forward and earn equal professional statuses.

SUSAN BRANDEIS

Susan Brandeis applies her knowledge of the textile products and methods that she began learning as a child to design artworks inspired by the environment. Brandeis explained: "I was a sponge for every textile technique I came across, enthusiastic about learning everything I could about creating beautiful and well-designed works" (Create Whimsy, n.d.). As a textile artist, Brandeis views herself as a craftsperson, artist, and designer given her applications of media, artistic ideas, and design processes. Her keen observation skills, attention to details, and creative connections as presented in her art articulate the importance of environmental awareness. She typically produces textile works using natural fibers, compared to synthetic ones that are non-eco-friendly. Brandeis's emphasis on creating beautiful environmentally-themed artworks sheds light on the benefits of being in nature and preserving natural places. She participates in fieldwork at breathtaking locations, makes sketches, and takes aerial photographs and close-up views to document the unique qualities of her chosen landscapes. Hiking has also played an important role in her creative process. It has provided her with access to out-of-the-way locations and enabled her to study the environment from different perspectives.

Over her career, Brandeis has developed the skills needed to manipulate textile media to produce a full range of textural surfaces and form dynamic designs that center on topographical landscapes. Because textiles are generally flexible and can be folded and/or pieced together, Brandeis has the ability to create art on the go, rather than needing to produce everything in her studio. Her works range from small and intimate to large-scale designs enriched with details and layers. *Aerial Dreamscape I*, a small-scale embroidery, combines the presence of a landscape with the sensation of a blissful dream (Figure 19.3). Its visual content feels expansive due to its bird's-eye view that gives the impression of looking

FIGURE 19.3 Susan Brandeis, *Aerial Dreamscape I*, 1980. Embroidered cotton broadcloth and cotton thread, 4 × 4 in. (10.2 × 10.2 cm).
Source: Smithsonian American Art Museum. © Susan Brandeis.

down at a serene rainbow-colored land-scape. Color patches become lighter in the distance and smaller to replicate aerial perspective. Rectangular segments produce dynamic rhythms that move viewers' eyes across the vibrant scene. *Aerial Dreamscape I's* grid pattern is reminiscent of the U.S. Public Land Survey that used linear markings on the earth's surface to subdivide land parcels. Its repetitive geometric design contrasts against the organic flow of a body of water that Brandeis represented by leaving sections of the white cotton broadcloth fabric unembroidered. Imagining nature's aesthetic qualities in the form of a textile dreamscape with pristine water flowing through, *Aerial Dreamscape I* embodies the tranquil sensations that arise when creating art and experiencing nature's aesthetic harmony in remarkable places.

BUILDING CREATIVE CONNECTIONS

Saar, Warashina, and Brandeis demonstrated the meaning of going places with symbols that included wings, wheels, and a bird's-eye view. Each artist specializes in different art media and approaches their subject matter in personalized ways. Saar teaches about desired changes in the weather and people's perceptions of race. Warashina demonstrates women's abilities to understand technical processes. Brandeis instructs society about nature's benefits and protecting its beauty. Their artworks cultivate positive changes. Knowledge of Saar's, Warashina's, and Brandeis's creative connections between art and life drives *Teaching and Learning in the STEAM Artist's Studio 19.1*. Its *STEAM Amplifiers* teach about drones.

Teaching and Learning in the STEAM Artist's Studio 19.1

Introduce students to the big idea of going places and refer to Saar's, Warashina's, and Brandeis's representations of going places and sites of engagement. Prompt students to describe and interpret the artworks' wings, wheels, and bird's-eye view symbols. Then, discuss how the artists have applied artistic skills to communicate ideas about change, equality, and nature in their chosen media.

Essential/Guiding Questions

1. What do people mean when they say a person is going places? Why is it important for people to feel like they are heading in the right direction in life? How did Saar, Warashina, and Brandeis achieve this as professional artists?
2. What role can artists play in reinforcing or swaying people's mindsets to move their positions on societal issues? What creative connections did Saar, Warashina, and Brandeis make to communicate important ideas through art?

Daily Learning Targets

As an artist, I can create artwork that teaches about the big idea of going places.

- I can experiment with art media and processes to plan my artwork.
- I can incorporate symbols that represent going places and make refinements to my work using the media and processes I have chosen.
- I can prepare my artwork for class presentation, describe its intent and make creative connections to the artists' examples I studied and the meaning of going places.

National Core Arts Anchor Standards NVAS 3, 5, 8, and 11.
www.nationalartsstandards.org

Teaching for Students' Development

PK-12: (A) Facilitate students' experimentation with art media using sketchbooks, learning centers, and demonstrations. (B) Reinforce the meaning of idioms including going places and STEAM idioms like once in a blue moon.

Early childhood: Young children need assistance in learning a figurative language. Teach them how an idiom's meaning differs from its literal meaning. Show pictures and repeat the phrase during class conversations. Assist students with the manipulation of art media and processes.

Middle childhood: Students are building skills in selecting words to communicate precise meanings. Have students practice using idioms correctly, such as going places, busy as a bee, and other STEAM idioms.

Early adolescence: Middle school students admire inspirational people and the work that they do. Ask students to make connections to how they plan to go places in their lives and inspire others using positive role models' examples.

Adolescence: High school students ponder their adult roles and the steps that they are taking and/or plan to take to get where they want to go in life. Ask students how positive choices can help them reach their goals and how people can take steps to correct negative ones and get back on track.

STEAM AMPLIFIERS CHOICE #1—DRONES, ART, AND SOCIETY

Drones, also known as **unmanned aircraft systems (UAS)**, are flying robots that range in size and purpose. Some are equipped with global positioning systems (GPS) that navigate their exact locations and lidar sensors to produce 3D images (see Chapter 4). Teaching drones in context, we can describe drones in contemporary society including artists' creations, scientific investigations, natural disaster surveillance, search and rescue missions, deliveries, and military operations. Drones

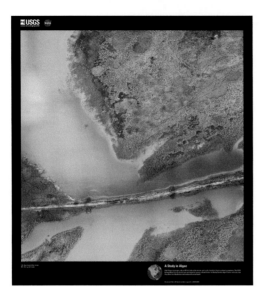

FIGURE 19.4 Scientists operate drones with multispectral sensors to study algal blooms.
Source: UAS. Public Domain.

can also provide inexpensive alternatives to accessing hard-to-reach places and ones that are hazardous to humans.

We can also teach creative connections between contemporary drone usage and this chapter's artists, as well as contemporary artists who create art about and with drones. For example, Brandeis's art presents bird's-eye views and close-up details of the earth's surface. The textural qualities in Figure 19.4 of an algal bloom are reminiscent of some of Brandeis's later designs. Students can use existing drone images and ones they photograph using drones as inspirations to create art in diverse media, such as textiles.

Drone journalism and **drone cinematography** have documented global protests that call for social justice and racial equality with footage that has captured how individuals have come together to advocate for positive changes. These examples align with Saar's call for change with her *Liberation of Aunt Jemima* assemblage. Drones can also apply Saar's *Wishing for*

Winter theme to capture drone-filmed winter landscapes to develop into artistic films and for scientific studies, including climate change.

In the 1960s, when Warashina began her career, ceramics was viewed as a man's profession. Warashina's *Convertible Car Kiln* symbolizes women's equality and proficiencies in understanding the technologies and production methods of clay, kilns, and glazes. Her art and professional experiences connect to the Women and Drones (n.d.) network, whose mission is "to increase female participation in the economic opportunities of the industry" and identified how men in 2020 earned 92.8% of the Federal Aviation Administration (FAA) remote pilot licenses (called Part 107, Small UAS rule to fly drones). To correct this imbalance, Women and Drones cultivate women's proficiencies in unmanned aircraft systems, urban air mobility, and advanced air mobility industries. It also offers educational workshops for teachers including drone curriculum development and provides teacher-incentive grants to access drones.

STEAM AMPLIFIERS CHOICE #2—AERODYNAMIC DRONE FLIGHTS

Students want to fly drones as part of their studies. The **quadcopter drone**, a multi-rotor drone with four propellors, is the most common drone used in schools (Figures 19.5 and 19.6). While many drones operate outdoors, some drones are designed for indoor use. To fly drones, students will need to become familiar with the drone's **flight controller**, which consists of circuit boards and sensors. It is

FIGURE 19.5 High school student John Mendoza operates a drone to produce paint splatters.
Source: Mike Mitchell, teacher.

described as the drone's brain. Many flight controllers include a **gyroscope** that measures the drone's rotation and stabilizes it when disrupted and an **accelerometer** that measures its acceleration. The flight controller receives input signals from the

FIGURE 19.6 Students fly drones at a one-week residence at the Oregon Institute of Technology. (cropped photograph)
Source: Oregon Department of Transportation. Flickr, (CC by 2.0).

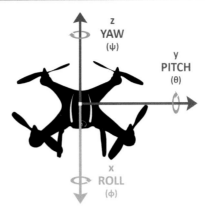

FIGURE 19.7 This drone diagram illustrates roll, pitch, and yaw.
Source: Compilation, Paige Brenner.

drone's **remote controller**, a receiver for operating the drone. Students can use a tablet, goggles, or smartphone to watch the drone's live video feed transmissions as it flies. This is called the **first-person view** (FPV).

Students benefit from learning about drones' aerodynamic qualities, safety procedures, and drone pilots' terminology. Figure 19.7 presents the drone's six degrees of freedom that illustrate its position and orientation as it flies in three-dimensional space. The x-, y-, and z-axes represent the drone's translational movements and intersect at the point of origin, the drone's center of gravity. The drone's rotational movements are called the roll, pitch, and yaw. The **roll** (φ angle) represents the drone's rotation on the x-axis. It identifies the drone's lateral movement in the left direction (called **negative roll**) and the right direction (called **positive roll**). To understand the movement, students can imagine the motions of their bodies or their pets rolling back and forth on their bellies, rolling in one direction and then the other. The **pitch** (θ angle) represents the drone's rotation on the y-axis and describes the drone's lateral movement with the drone's nose (front side) tilting downward to move forward (called the **positive pitch**) and the nose tilting upward to move backward (called the **negative pitch**). Students can compare the drone's movement to a water pitcher moving downward to pour water and lifting it back up to stop the water from flowing. The **yaw** (ψ angle) represents the drone's rotation on the z-axis. It describes the rotational motion that moves the drone in clockwise and counterclockwise directions. It produces the drone's circular motions. A **positive yaw** turns the drone to the right and a **negative yaw** turns the drone to the left. Students can envision how the yaw's movements are similar to a door opening and closing.

The **throttle** is the vertical movement that moves the drone up (called the **positive throttle**) or down (called the **negative throttle**). It determines the drone's speed. The drone's angled propellers spin and push air down to push the drone up to fly. Several instructional videos demonstrate drones performing these motions.

In addition to watching these rotational movements through instructional videos and drones in flight, students can also practice using their bodies to replicate the roll, pitch, and yaw movements. These activities help students demystify the mathematical modeling of Figure 19.7.

MOVING FULL STEAM AHEAD...

This chapter aligned artworks by Saar, Warashina, and Brandeis using the artistic behavior of making creative connections with the themes of going places and sites of engagement to address personal interests and societal issues. It completes Part VI and this book's *Artists' Lessons to Thrive!* chapters. Part VII of this book is titled *"Moving Full STEAM Ahead: Exciting Adventures Await Us...."* It contains Chapter 20 that teaches about great STEAM teaching and learning in practice.

References

Create Whimsy. (n.d.). *Spotlight: Susan Brandeis, textile artist.* https://createwhimsy.com/projects/spotlight-susan-brandeis-textile-artist/

Jeck, D. (2005, September 8). *Oral history interview with Patti Warashina, 2005 September 8.* Archives of American Art, Smithsonian Institution. https://www.aaa.si.edu/collections/interviews/oral-history-interview-patti-warashina-12864-transcript

MoAD. [Museum of the African Diaspora]. (2018, November 27). *Betye Saar: Lifetime achievement in the arts—MoAD Afropolitan Ball, 2017.* [Video] YouTube. https://www.youtube.com/watch?v=2L3Yk3Jfga8

Smithsonian American Art Museum. (n.d.). *Convertible Kiln Car.* https://americanart.si.edu/artwork/convertible-car-kiln-33915

Women and Drones. (n.d.). *About Women and Drones.* https://womenanddrones.com/about/

PART VII

Moving Full STEAM Ahead

Exciting Adventures Await Us...

Chapter 20

Meet the Educators

Great STEAM Teaching and Learning in Practice!

FIGURE 20.1 Creating these STEAM tunnel books exemplified the processes of learning from experts, taking risks, growing from mistakes, and applying transdisciplinary STEAM content, artists' inspirations, quality design, and artistic behaviors.

Source: © Debrah Sickler-Voigt, Paige Brenner & Richard Sickler. Photo: Richard Sickler.

STEAM Teaching and Learning Through the Arts and Design: A Practical Guide for PK–12 Educators has provided us with pathways to conjoin disciplines to implement interdisciplinary/transdisciplinary STEAM studies that link artists' teachings, creative behaviors, and ways of knowing (Figure 20.1). We learned how the *Artists' Lessons to Thrive!* choice-based lessons reinforce the professional practices and mindsets that STEAM professionals employ. Their lessons' guiding questions, learning targets, and *STEAM Amplifiers*

offered us rich content and context to eliminate stereotypical, diluted, and/or subservient arts and design integrations.

Putting this book's exemplars into practice, we can encourage students to make curricular choices, explore diverse media and processes, take leadership roles, and activate the artistic behaviors of idea development, observation, imagination and wonderment, persistence, and making creative connections. The following selections of educators' best and inclusive practices reinforce what we have learned

DOI: 10.4324/9781003183693-27

about STEAM teaching and learning through the arts and design. All quotes result from personal communications with the educators in 2022.

MODELING PLANNING AND INSTRUCTION THROUGH STEAM STANDARDS: CATHY SMILAN

Standards play a prominent role in Cathy Smilan's conceptual model for STEAM planning and instruction. Smilan emphasizes the necessity of "creating a proper space where the visual arts are securely placed" as a coequal STEAM discipline. Educators need to know and understand STEAM disciplines' standards to incorporate them into their planning. Standards reinforce the arts' essential role in the curriculum and teach shared curricular concepts that build students' interdisciplinary/transdisciplinary understandings. Given educators' reviews of the standards and preliminary planning, Smilan formulates guiding questions to further develop their ideas so that they can design STEAM lessons with credible interdisciplinary/transdisciplinary connections. She asks: "What is it that you need to know in order to teach this lesson?" "What are your resources—including other faculty members?" She then challenges them to identify the most effective instructional methods and lesson procedures to teach diversified students. Smilan also meets with educators individually to assist them in bridging information gaps, securing new knowledge, and establishing partnerships.

Educators internalize these practices of authentic art integration and identify learning as an ongoing process. Smilan emphasizes that educators also need to advocate for themselves as "leaders within the school community so that administrators understand how valuable the arts are within STEM.... We show them how important our objectives and standards are." Her holistic approach to STEAM planning and instruction models best practices for educators and sparks their curiosities in wanting to know more (see Smilan & Siegesmund, 2023).

Personally Driven Entry Points to STEAM Instruction and Assessment: Richard Siegesmund

Richard Siegesmund designs approaches to STEAM instruction and assessment that, drawing on numeric data sets and statistical analysis, foster qualitative decision-making with data visualizations in the forms of infographics and two- and three-dimensional artworks. Siegesmund also has teachers and students reflect on how STEAM-driven visual work generates critical thinking skills. Data analysis reaches beyond indisputable true or false statistical findings. It raises questions; it promotes discussions. He facilitates idea development by encouraging teachers and students to explore issues and concerns that they find personally compelling. He promotes constructive discourse emphasizing the interconnectedness of STEAM's disciplines.

Siegesmund advocates that well-designed STEAM lessons and assessments demonstrate Elliot Eisner's (1998) pedagogical principle of flexible purposing. This occurs when teachers and students seize opportunities that arise in the course of a lesson to take teaching and learning to new outcomes that were not initially anticipated at the beginning. This promotes investing in student work, using what both teachers and students deeply value because they care about their work, not just their grades.

Reflecting on the outcomes, his students often tell Siegesmund "I want to come back and do it again. It says something about me." Such examples demonstrate the importance of teachers and students engaging and taking ownership of the process of STEAM teaching, learning, and assessment. These intrinsically-driven behaviors cannot be captured and motivated by grades alone (see Smilan & Siegesmund, 2023).

EVALUATING STEAM SCHOOL DESIGNATION PROGRAMS: MABEL MORALES AND KIRSTIE MARTINEZ

Miami-Dade County Public Schools (2022) year-long STE(A)M School Designation Program's aim is "to ensure our community has the next generation of inventors, explorers, innovators, artists and leaders" (para. 1). Mabel Morales, District Supervisor for the Visual and Performing Arts, and Kirstie Martinez, Curriculum Support Specialist/STEAM Visual Arts Liaison, lead its visual-arts program and provide teacher professional developments and facilitate hands-on learning with community partners.

FIGURE   20.2 Jenny   Llewellyn-Jones' display presents her middle school students' studies designing a 3D prototype for a hurricane and flood-resistant house with the Tinkercad app. Her display includes students' use of computers and a 3D printer.

Each participating teacher creates a bulletin board/table display of works that document how students have acquired in-depth understandings of interconnected STEAM subject matter during an academic year. This K-12 initiative produces a wealth of innovative student outcomes with lessons that apply different standards, media, and technologies (Figures 20.2–20.4).

Morales and Martinez conduct multiple classroom visits to provide teachers with feedback to assist them in understanding

FIGURE   20.3 Augusto Zambrana's elementary students produced a freestanding wire structure with melted wax crayons that documents the physical and chemical changes of wax with applied heat.

FIGURE 20.4 Patty Keller's "high school students produced a wave sculpture made from recycled materials that follow the Golden Ratio. It documents how nature's curvilinear forms can inspire aesthetic designs and ocean waves are a perfect example of the golden ratio manifesting in nature."

the criteria needed to receive maximum points on the district's 5.0 STEAM matrix. Teachers' STEAM displays document students' learning processes from brainstorming preliminary ideas to final designs and include written reflections, photographs, and videos that record student growth. Morales and Martinez evaluate the displays to measure the levels of students' deep learning and higher-order thinking in alignment with grade-level STEAM standards. Participating in the program, Morales and Martinez affirm: "The students benefit because the processes are being mirrored in the content area classrooms as well as the arts classroom resulting in a better correlation to learning across the disciplines."

REMOVING BOUNDARIES IN STEAM EDUCATION: YICHIEN COOPER

Yichien Cooper designed her STEAM model to remove barriers by focusing on reflective teaching and learning processes. Integrated STEAM studies "leverage the intersections between disciplinary subjects, subjects and learners, and learners and their social, cultural, and economic surroundings for deep and sustainable learning." Speaking English as her second language, Cooper processes information and ideas by forming symbolic meanings and metaphors and has applied them to teach STEAM. Thresholds represent transitions. Like stepping over the threshold at a gateway's entry point, Cooper identifies the threshold as a symbol that embodies the boundaries that the different STEAM disciplines represent. STEAM is a "pathway to dialogue that makes things relatable" and encourages critical thinking, builds bridges between disciplines, and forms dynamic relationships. The STEAM curriculum reaches far beyond technology and media arts integration. It erases subjects' boundaries and conjoins disciplinary content to form multifaceted understandings.

Cooper's model is inspired by Anderson and Milbrandt's (2005) *Art for Life* philosophy that emphasizes the values of authentic teaching and learning that has relevance in life. Teachers and students visualize the joys of STEAM as they make personal connections to curricular content. It also addresses timely issues, including social justice, equity, and inclusion to spark honest dialog about issues that have real-world implications (see Cooper, 2017; Cooper & Lai, 2023). Given its effectiveness, Cooper's model has been adopted by a Taiwanese elementary school that received government support to become the nation's first STEAM center.

FACILITATING STEAM MINDSETS USING THE COLORS OF THE WORLD: JAMES WELLS

As Education Manager for Crayola, James Wells leads professional developments that emphasize STEAM professionals' mindsets including problem finding, problem solving, recognizing patterns, utilizing divergent thinking skills, and producing innovative designs. His professional developments explain how STEAM professionals make changes and refinements as they work toward desired outcomes. They invent new ideas and improve existing inventions with innovative ideas that are better designed, more efficient, less wasteful, and/or more cost-effective.

Wells's professional developments incorporate Crayola's Colors of the World project—a real-world STEAM improvement that consists of product colors that are representative of all people's skin tones (Figure 20.5). Crayola partnered with Victor Casale, former Chief Chemist for MAC Cosmetics and CEO and Cofounder of MOB Beauty, as their lead scientist and product developer, given his expertise in developing skin tones for the cosmetic industry. To name its colors, Crayola classified people's skin tones as light, medium, and deep and identified the undertones underneath the skin's surface as rose, almond, and golden. Wells teaches educators how students can apply observation skills to find their perfect match by comparing their skin to the colors on the box to draw themselves in the roles of STEAM professionals—such as a marine engineer (Figure 20.6). Given these constructive mindsets, Wells encourages all children to envision themselves as innovative STEAM creators, who can solve the world's problems—just like Crayola did by developing its Colors of the World project.

ACCESSING STEAM WITH ASSISTIVE TECHNOLOGIES: MONICA LEISTER, JOSHUA HARPER, AND ALLEN HUANG

Teaching STEAM to students with visual impairments ages 7–21 at the Tennessee School for the Blind (TSB), Monica Leister introduced stop-motion animation into her curriculum because it aligns with her

FIGURE 20.5 Wells's children draw self-portraits using Crayola's Colors of the World.

FIGURE 20.6 Wells's son enjoys sketching ship designs given his interest in marine engineering.

multisensory approach to teaching with its fusion of tactile visual art materials and media arts. Under Leister's guidance, the students develop original STEAM-inspired storylines and construct sets, characters, and props. Leister works with a team of educators to provide students with necessary assistive technologies. Technology educator, Joshua Harper, describes "assistive technology at TSB is how our kids access everything." The school's Director of Accessible Instructional Materials, Allen Huang, trains teachers and students how to use assistive technologies ranging from low-tech to high-tech options, such as magnification tools, screen readers, and braille displays, to foster student independence. He explains "assistive technology is primarily all about providing access." It includes equipment, systems, and services that enable students to participate and perform equally in learning tasks.

Harper collaborates with Leister by teaching 3D-printing methods and developing sound recordings with the students using high-tech mobile equipment, as exemplified in their stop-motion animation *Where Are the Bees?* (Figures 11.7 and 20.7) that features student narrations

FIGURE 20.7 This K-12 stop-motion animation frame illustrates the dangers of pesticides to bees. *Source: Monica Leister, Joshua Harper, and author, instructors. Background photo by Jordan Cormack on Unsplash.*

and sound effects—including buzzing bees, a spray canister, and a rocket ship. Given their access to exemplary instruction and assistive technologies, the students exhibit their stop-motion animations internationally and have received international honorable mentions and diplomatic recognition for their achievements.

MUSEUM-LED PROFESSIONAL DEVELOPMENTS FOR ARTS- AND STEAM-INFUSION: ALLISON ROSS, ANNE HENDERSON, SHAUN GILES, AND KATHERINE WEBB

Metro Nashville Public School's Visual Arts Coordinator Allison Ross values the *U.S. Department of Education Professional Development Arts Educators Grant* her district received with the Frist Art Museum because it ensures "the equitable distribution of materials and equipment to students and teachers" in her district's Title I Schools and provides arts- and STEAM-infused professional developments. Frist Art Museum's Anne Henderson, Director of Education and Engagement, and Shaun Giles, Community Engagement Director, contributed to the grant writing and designed its professional developments. The grant funds teacher workshops, museum field trips, artist mentors, and iPads for students to create movies and animations.

Henderson explained how her team is achieving the grant's aim of improving professional practices and providing instructional resources, assessments, and technologies by "ensuring that teachers are engaged and learning new strategies, and understanding how to integrate the museum resources with their teaching." For example, their professional developments teach educators Housen & Yenawin's (2001) Visual Thinking Strategies for students to build critical thinking skills as they analyze art. Giles reflected: "The idea of community sharing knowledge, sharing the value of the arts, the value of problem solving that comes with critical thinking is important as we continue to advance beyond our generation to the next." Summarizing her experiences, elementary teacher Katherine Webb resonated with the Visual Thinking Strategies derived question: "What do you see?" Rather than giving students the answers, Webb expressed "Its open-ended approach is more powerful because students are the ones that are connecting dots. It's a very simple but very powerful takeaway."

FIGURE 20.8 Levar Robinson applies his knowledge of the visual and performing arts to teach STEAM.

STEAM-DRIVEN COMMUNITY ARTS EDUCATION: LEVAR ROBINSON

"I always tell the kids: Go big!" explained Levar Robinson, who showcases students' talents through community art education including mural designs, chalk art, gardening, and performances (Figure 20.8). STEAM integration comes natural to Robinson, who has taught middle school science, special education, and art. His lessons instill: "The scientific method and art process are the same things. You get an idea and you're going to try it out and see what works. What doesn't work, go back and revise it." His classroom and community-based conversations build

connections between STEAM and life. When developing spray-painted murals, Robinson demonstrates how the process is similar to airbrushing. He makes comparisons to working with layers in Photoshop and how laser printers print multiple layers to develop final products.

Robinson pulls from his own middle school experience in home economics to build students' confidence. "I was one of the kids that didn't fit in—the first black kid and everything and … one of the poorest kids in school." He recognized how his creative skills brought him positive recognition and built his confidence: "I could do everything!" Striving to build students' confidence, Robinson's lessons begin with smaller tasks before moving into larger ones so that students can work through challenges. His instructional methods place students at the heart of their community and provide them with "a feeling that somebody is caring about them. Somebody sees that work [they are doing]. And, they start doing more!"

TEACHING ARTISTS SOARING STEAM EDUCATION TO NEW HEIGHTS: MIKE MITCHELL AND MAHWISH CHISHTY

High school teaching-artist Mike Mitchell invited Mahwish Chishty, a Pakistani-American teaching-artist (Figure 20.9), who creates multimedia drone-themed art to collaborate on an exhibition titled *This Is Our War.* Chishty's drone inspirations began when she learned news reports that confirmed that American drone strikes killed over 300 Pakistani civilians and heard that the U.S. Government denied any civilian casualties. Wanting students to analyze the truth when hearing conflicting reports, Mitchell asked 200-participating students guiding questions to link Chishty's art with their life in a community that Mitchell and his students described as overpoliced. Mitchell explained that his students "understood being at the wrong place at the wrong time," and how unwarranted arrests, violence, and loss of life have impacted innocent civilians. Their exhibition included student-splatter paintings created with the school's Parrot Bebop drone and

FIGURE 20.10 High school students created a drone-inspired installation with tiles.
Source: Mike Mitchell and Mahwish Chishty, teachers.

a 200-tile drone-shaped installation (Figure 20.10). Chishty illuminated how the aerial view of their installation "is the opposite of what happens in reality" because drones can appear invisible to civilians looking up at the sky. In contrast, Chishty's drones are highly visible.

Given their STEAM collaboration, Mitchell and Chishty have taught students to seek truth and use persistence to broaden their perspectives and reach academic heights. Mitchell continues to build community-based STEAM collaborations and Chishty has since developed international collaborations with schoolchildren that address border cultures and conflict resolution.

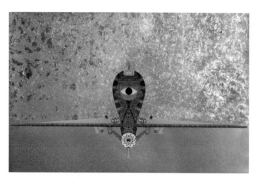

FIGURE 20.9 Mahwish Chishty, 2015, *Reaper*, Gouache and gold flakes on paper, 30″ × 20″ (76 cm × 51 cm).
Source: © Mahwish Chishty.

NURTURING EMOTIONAL INTELLIGENCE THROUGH STEAM: ADRIANA CASTRO-GARCIA, KAITLYN ESTES, MENLEY SAYLOR, AND LUCY LANGWORTHY

Collaborating with liberal arts and science majors, preservice teachers Adriana Castro-Garcia, Kaitlyn Estes, and Menley Saylor took leadership roles developing murals representing the 2020 World

Economic Forum's soft skills students need for career success for Middle Tennessee State University's (MTSU's) Arts and Sciences Majors Showcase (Figure 20.11). Project coordinator, Lucy Langworthy explained, "students named this mural project *Be the Missing Piece* and used the puzzle piece shape to illustrate the ten skills and show students that they could be the missing piece if they developed these skills."

Having graduated and transitioned into first-year teaching during the COVID-19 pandemic, Castro-Garcia, Estes, and Saylor reflected on their applications of the skills. Estes emphasized the importance of emotional intelligence in teaching: "Emotionally you have to be prepared to handle so many things." Castro-Garcia and Saylor agreed and the three described how they applied emotional intelligence to comfort and support children experiencing pandemic-related hardships and bullying. Their modeling of emotional intelligence in STEAM teaching and learning benefits students and demonstrates

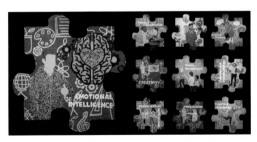

FIGURE 20.11 MTSU's Arts and Sciences Majors Showcase's *Be the Missing Piece* murals (5′ × 5′ each) feature the 2020 World Economic Forum's soft skills. They include complex problem-solving, critical thinking, creativity, people management, coordinating with others, emotional intelligence, judgment and decision-making, service orientation, negotiation, and cognitive flexibility.

Source: Author, professor and Lucy Langworthy, coordinator. MTSU's MT Engage Grant.

how they achieved MTSU's project goals. Langworthy explained:

> Castro-Garcia, Estes, and Saylor felt empowered with the introduction to the soft skills they received at MTSU and the opportunity to put them into action. In fact, they, like many others on our campus, have suggested that these skills should no longer be referred to as "soft skills." They will be *essential* skills for professional success in today's schools and workforce.

STEAM MINDSETS IN THE NON-SCHOOL HOURS: HENRY AND IRIS LAU

"Free your mind" are words of wisdom that guide learning and hone students' innovative mindsets at Henry and Iris Lau's *Simply Art*, an after-school art program based in Hong Kong that serves 300 students ages 4–21. The Lau's worked as professional architects before founding *Simply Art* and have integrated their expert knowledge of the built environment into *Simply Art's* curriculum. Students learn about humanity's deeply-rooted relationships to the environment and make personal correlations by reflecting on their life experiences and STEAM studies. The Lau's explained:

> We all are living in an everchanging society which all people are facing different problems every day. All those problems are going to reconstruct our living style, cultural development, thinking direction, our future, outlook of our planet earth…. We need to sync with all those changes.

FIGURE 20.12 Lau You Gi, (11 years old), *Chemistry.*
Source: Simply Art, Hong Kong, China. ICEFA Lidice 47ᵗʰ Exhibition.

Heightened sensitivities become ingrained in the learning process. Students independently collect research data; produce conceptual drawings; and analyze their work before meeting with the Lau's for feedback. This process facilitates students' original idea development. Students continue to make observations, listen, ask questions, share their opinions, and make refinements to their work. Outcomes produce "sensations of visual magic and excitement in their hearts," as demonstrated in Figure 20.12 that illustrates a traditional indigo dying process resulting from organic chemistry, and Figure 20.13's

FIGURE 20.13 Lau Kin Gi, (15 years old), *Robots.*
Source: Simply Art, Hong Kong, China. ICEFA Lidice 49ᵗʰ Exhibition.

futuristic robot-infused built environment. *Simply Art's* students have received international recognition and awards for their work resulting from the Lau's exemplary teaching, advocacy, and community outreach.

MOVING FULL STEAM AHEAD: EXCITING ADVENTURES AWAIT US...

This book showcased the intrinsic rewards of great STEAM teaching and learning in practice through its choice-based interdisciplinary/transdisciplinary lessons, artistic behaviors, and educators' insightful perspectives. Applying its information and our existing knowledge, we are prepared to move full STEAM ahead in STEAM planning, instruction, and assessment to suit our particular teaching styles and student learning needs. Exciting adventures await us!

CHAPTER QUESTIONS AND ACTIVITIES

1. Summarize what you have learned about interdisciplinary/transdisciplinary STEAM teaching and learning through the arts and design.
2. Which model artists, lessons, and educators' practices stood out to you the most? How do they correlate with your teaching and student-learning needs?
3. What are your immediate and long-term plans for applying best and inclusive practices for interdisciplinary/transdisciplinary STEAM teaching and learning?

References

Anderson, T., & Milbrandt, M. (2005). *Art for life.* McGraw Hill.

Cooper, Y., & Lai, A. (2023). *Intersections and thresholds of STEAM education.* Sense/Brill.

Eisner, E. (1998). *The enlightened eye.* Merrill.

Housen, A., & Yenawine, P. (2001). *Basic VTS at a glance.* https://web.archive.org/web/20111124102840/http://www.vtshome.org/system/resources/0000/0018/basic_vts_at_a_glance.pdf

Miami-Dade County Public Schools. (2022). *Division of Academics-STEAM.* https://steam.dadeschools.net/#!/fullWidth/1860

Smilan, C., & Siegesmund, R. (2023). *Authentic secondary arts assessment: Snapshots from art teacher practice.* Routledge.

陳怡倩 [Cooper, Y. (2017). *The power of integrated curriculum: The core of STEAM education.* Hunan Publishing.

For Product Safety Concerns and Information please contact our
EU representative GPSR@taylorandfrancis.com Taylor & Francis
Verlag GmbH, Kaufingerstraße 24, 80331 München, Germany